The North Carolina
Birding Trail
Coastal Plain Trail Guide

Welcome to
The North Carolina Birding Trail!

A Birding Paradise

North Carolina harbors an incredible diversity of habitats, including coastal estuaries, longleaf pine savannas, and spruce-fir forests. These habitats provide food and shelter for more than 440 bird species throughout the year, making North Carolina a premiere destination for birders and nature-lovers. The North Carolina Birding Trail is a driving trail to link birders and nature-based tourists with great birding sites across the state and the local communities in which they are found. So get out and explore our great state and the birding treasures it holds!

Table of Contents

Copyright © 2007 North Carolina Birding Trail
ISBN 978-0-9794468-0-1

Cover design, book design and layout by Chuck Samuels, Design Dimension, Inc. Raleigh, North Carolina

Printed in North Carolina by Theo Davis Printing

Printed on recycled paper

About Us

The North Carolina Birding Trail is a partnership among six agencies and organizations in North Carolina. Our mission is *"to conserve and enhance North Carolina's bird habitat by promoting sustainable bird watching activities, economic opportunities and conservation education."*

Audubon North Carolina's mission is to help conserve and restore the North Carolina habitats we share with all wildlife, focusing on the needs of birds.

North Carolina Cooperative Extension is an educational partnership helping people put research-based knowledge to work for economic prosperity, environmental stewardship and an improved quality of life.

The mission of **North Carolina Sea Grant** is to enhance the sustainable use and conservation of ocean and coastal resources to benefit communities, the economy and the environment.

The mission of the **State Parks** system is to conserve and protect representative examples of the natural beauty, ecological features and recreational resources of statewide significance; to provide outdoor recreational opportunities in a safe and healthy environment; and to provide environmental education opportunities that promote stewardship of the state's natural heritage.

The mission of the **North Carolina Wildlife Resources Commission** is to manage, restore, develop, cultivate, conserve, protect, and regulate wildlife resources and their habitats for the citizens of the state.

The **U.S. Fish and Wildlife Service's** mission is working with others, to conserve, protect and enhance fish, wildlife, and plants and their habitats for the continuing benefit of the American people.

Beyond these six core participating organizations, the North Carolina Birding Trail would like to thank the following supporters for their financial contributions to this publication:

Acknowledgments

We also would like to extend our thanks to the many people who helped complete this publication by writing site descriptions, editing text, providing design advice and donating photographs. The following people or organizations have provided assistance: David Allen, Scott Anderson, Nate Bacheler, Brady Beck, Marie Boucher, Mark Buckler, Alan Cradick, Jim Craig, Salinda Daley, Craig Ellison, John Ennis, Lena Gallitano, Walker Golder, Mark Johns, Jeff Lewis, Sean McElhone, Chris Moorman, NC Coastal Federation, NC National Estuarine Research Reserve, Joe Peacos Jr., Chrissy Pearson, Cory Redick, Phil Rhyne, Harry Sell, Andy Wood. The Cardinal Foundation and the North Carolina Department of Commerce have also provided key support to the North Carolina Birding Trail.

Welcome and Introduction

Coastal Plain Trail Guide

This guide, the first of three regional North Carolina Birding Trail guides, presents the traveler with 102 birding sites, in 16 groupings across the North Carolina coastal plain - areas east of Interstate 95. Each group is complete with a map and includes site descriptions for each birding destination, as well as useful information about other community attractions you'll find along the way. While the groups have been designed to cluster sites that are within easy travel distances of one another, it is not necessary to travel the North Carolina Birding Trail in any particular order. Directions to each site are given from the nearest major state or federal highway.

Planning Your Visit

Before you visit...

Be sure to review the following list of useful tips to make your travels more enjoyable.

1. Plan to provide your own food and drink while visiting sites along the Trail. Few sites provide concessions. In addition, some rural areas may have limited services, such as gas stations and restaurants, so plan accordingly.
2. Plan ahead to visit sites that require advanced permission, a ferry ride, or that are boat accessible only.
3. Check the Carolina Bird Club's Rare Bird Alert web site (www.carolinabirdclub.org) for rare bird sightings and be sure to study up on the birds of North Carolina.
4. Consult birding resources ahead of time to optimize your chances of seeing seasonal target species. The key to successful birding is being in the right place at the right time of year.
5. Some sites support not only great birds, but also biting insects and the occasional venomous snake. Wear appropriate clothing and footwear and be sure to pack insect repellent and sunscreen.
6. Plan for variable weather and dress accordingly.
7. Be aware that some publicly owned lands are open to hunting during certain times of the year. Review the Hunting Areas inset on this page.

Hunting Areas:

On all public Game Lands, and in some national forests, national wildlife refuges, and other state-owned lands, birders must be aware of hunting seasons and regulations and should consult the most current version of the *North Carolina Inland Fishing, Hunting, and Trapping Regulations Digest* before visiting. Other useful Game Lands resources include the *Special Permit Hunts* book and the *Game Lands Map Book*. These books are usually available where hunting and fishing licenses are sold. Or visit www.ncwildlife.org to request such information. Sunday visitation of Game Lands is encouraged during hunting seasons as Sunday hunting is currently prohibited on Game Lands in North Carolina. See the Site Index in the back of the guide for a list of sites that allow hunting.

Paddle Trails:

If paddling on a North Carolina Birding Trail site, be sure to observe safe paddling techniques. Carry and use necessary safety gear for the outing. Visit the NC Paddle Trails Association web site (www.ncpaddletrails.org) for more paddle trail information. See the Site Index in the back of the guide for a list of sites that are paddle trail accessible.

Local community and business support

Successful birding trails also provide economic development opportunities for the local communities that host visiting birders. The following are some tips on how you can encourage local community and business support for the NC Birding Trail:

1. Educate local businesses and communities about the importance of birding areas.
2. Support communities and businesses displaying the "Birder Friendly" logo.
3. Leave the enclosed "Birder Calling Cards" at local establishments to identify yourself at the places you patronize.
4. Be friendly and courteous to local residents.

North Carolina Birding Trail
mountains • piedmont • coast

NC Birding Trail
NC Wildlife Resources Commission
1722 Mail Service Center
Raleigh, NC 27699-1722
(919) 604-5183
www.ncbirdingtrail.org
info@ncbirdingtrail.org

I stopped by because of the North Carolina Birding Trail.

Other birding resources

Consult the following books or web sites for additional information about birding sites in the North Carolina coastal plain. See the Site Index in the back of the guide for a listing of sites referenced in these sources.

- *A Birder's Guide to Coastal North Carolina*, John O. Fussell III. 1994. The University of North Carolina Press.
- *Birding North Carolina*, edited by Marshall Brooks and Mark Johns. 2005. Falcon Guide, The Globe Pequot Press.
- *Birding NC State Parks*, edited by Karen Bearden. 2002. Audubon North Carolina. *North Carolina Wildlife Viewing Guide*, Charles E. Roe. 1992. Falcon Press.
- The Carolina Bird Club web site: www.carolinabirdclub.org.

Top viewing techniques

Use the following techniques to maximize your opportunities to view birds in a natural setting while minimizing disturbance to the birds or their habitats.

1. Study your field guide ahead of time to familiarize yourself with the species in an area.
2. Scan for movement; move slowly and quietly.
3. Use a viewing blind and take advantage of natural cover.
4. Wear clothing that blends with the surroundings – except during hunting seasons, when blaze orange is a safety must.
5. Locate birds with your eyes, then focus in using binoculars, a scope, or a photo lens.
6. Listen for bird calls and songs; many birds will be detected by ear before they can be spotted by sight.
7. Leave your pets at home to reduce disturbance.

Respect the resources

Please use the following guidelines when visiting sites along the North Carolina Birding Trail.

1. Limit the use of recordings and other methods of attracting birds, and never use such methods in heavily birded areas, or for attracting any rare species.
2. Keep well back from nests and nesting colonies, roosts, display areas, and important feeding sites. Respect all posted signs, fencing, and instructions.
3. Do not feed or bait any wildlife.
4. Stay on existing roads, trails, and paths where possible; keep habitat disturbance to a minimum.
5. Respect the law and the rights of others. Do not enter private property without the owner's explicit permission.
6. Follow all laws, rules, and regulations governing use of roads and public areas.
7. Close gates and leave areas as you found them.
8. Practice common courtesy in contacts with other people. Your exemplary behavior will generate goodwill with birders and non-birders alike.
9. Be aware that some publicly owned lands are open to hunting during certain times of the year. See the previous page for more about Hunting Areas.

For more information, review the American Birding Association's Principles of Birding Ethics (http://americanbirding.org).

Using the Guide

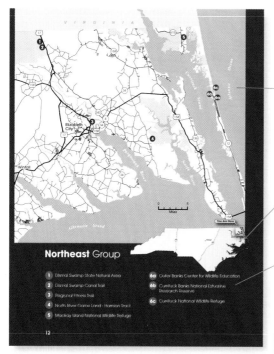

Map – Each color-coded section of the guide begins with a map depicting the locations of all the Birding Trail sites in that group. Use these maps, in combination with the written directions in each site description, to navigate to sites. All maps are north-oriented. Smaller inset maps are also provided at the start of each site description, as a quick reference. A map of the entire coastal plain region can be found on page 10, and on the inside back cover.

Thumbnail Map – Use this map to locate the group within the state.

Site Listing – All sites within the group are listed here in numerical order.

Singing Worm-eating Warbler

Key to map symbols and icons

 Interstate

 US Highway

 NC Highway

 NC Birding Trail site

 Managed public land**

Municipality

 Water

**These lands include National Forests, State Game Lands, National Seashores, National Wildlife Refuges, State Parks, or other federally or state owned lands.

Local Site Map – A close-up view of the site and surrounding area.

Site Information – Pertinent contact information, including the site owner or manager, street address or location, phone number, and web address (if available).

While You're In The Area – This section lists local cultural, historical, or community attractions to visit while traveling along this group of Birding Trail sites.

Site Description – A detailed description of the site, including recommendations on where to go in search of birds.

Sunset over Currituck Sound

While You're In the Area

Currituck Beach Lighthouse
Currituck Heritage Park
Corolla, NC 27927
252-453-8152
www.currituckbeachlight.com

Currituck – Knotts Island Ferry
NC Department of Transportation, Ferry Division
252-232-2683
www.ncdot.org/transit/ferry

Great Dismal Swamp National Wildlife Refuge
US Fish and Wildlife Service
3100 Desert Road
Suffolk, VA 23434
757-986-3705
www.fws.gov/northeast/greatdismalswamp

(continues)

Tricolored Heron

Northeast Group

21

③

Regional Fitness Trail

Site Information:
Contact: College of the Albemarle and
Albemarle Hospital
1208 North Road Street, Elizabeth City,
NC 27906
Pasquotank County
252-335-0821 x 2211

About the Site:
As you drive into this site, watch for the entrance to the 0.5 mile long boardwalk on the left side of the street by the campus buildings, identified as the College of the Albemarle Fenwick-Hollowell Wetlands Trail. From this entrance, the boardwalk takes you through a wet area with uprooted trees and thick vegetation that provides suitable habitat for cardinals, flycatchers, vireos and other songbirds. A short distance later, you emerge onto a canal that leads to the wide expanse of the Pasquotank River. Along the canal, there are good viewing opportunities for both resident and migrating songbirds. Watch for Green Heron and other wading birds at the water's edge. As the trail reaches the Pasquotank River, search the cypress trees hanging with Spanish moss for additional species. Watch for a beaver dam where the canal meets the river. Benches and gazebos along the river provide opportunities to sit quietly, listen and observe. The gazebos are home to Barn Swallow during the summer. Along the river a stand of phragmites provides habitat and cover that can be searched for additional species.

Snowy Egret

Species of Interest: Prothonotary Warbler, wading birds

Habitats: pine/hardwood forest, isolated wetlands, marsh, river

Access & Parking: From the entrance, drive to the back of the college and park in the overflow parking area away from the buildings. Access the boardwalk where the woods and swamp border the college to the north. Open daily during daylight hours. Restrooms are available at the college.

Directions: From the intersection of US 17 and US 158 in Elizabeth City, travel approximately 1 mile north to the college entrance on the east side of the road, just past the Albemarle Hospital.

Coordinates: N 36°19'32" W 76°13'05"
DeLorme (NC Gazetteer) Page: 26

15

Site Amenity Icons – A listing of amenities available on site. A key to the site amenity icons can be found on page 10, and inside the back cover.

Other Site Details – Additional information about the site, including species of interest, habitats present, access and parking details, and directions. Latitude and longitude coordinates of the site parking area are also listed, along with the relevant NC Gazetteer page.

Pay Special Attention to...
Be sure to review the site description in advance of your visit so that you can plan for any special considerations, including sites that:
1. require advanced notice or are by appointment only,
2. charge an entrance fee or have limited access hours,
3. allow hunting - see page 4 for more about Hunting Areas, or
4. are boat accessible only.

The Site Index in the back of the guide is a useful reference for this type of information.

Site Listing

Site Listing

Site Listing

Overall Site Map

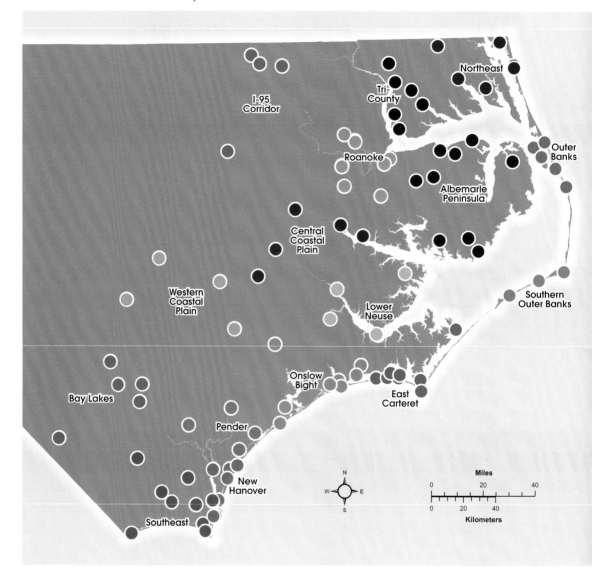

Key To Site Amenity Icons

Boat Access Only · Boat Launch · Camping · Fee · Handicap Access · Hiking Trails · Hunting · Interpretive Programs · Picnic Area · Restrooms · Trail Maps/Information · Viewing Platforms · Visitor Center

Welcome to the
Northeast Group

This corner of North Carolina is characterized by charming, historic towns and the water features they were built around: the Pasquotank River, the North River, and the Currituck Sound. Once a remote haven for waterfowl hunters and fishermen, visitors can now drive to the "end of the road" on the northernmost section of the Outer Banks. Inland of Currituck Sound, small towns and cities attract travelers with their historic appeal and wonderful cultural attractions that interpret the rich heritage of the region.

You Are Here

77

Raleigh

95

Northeast Group

© Mark Buckler

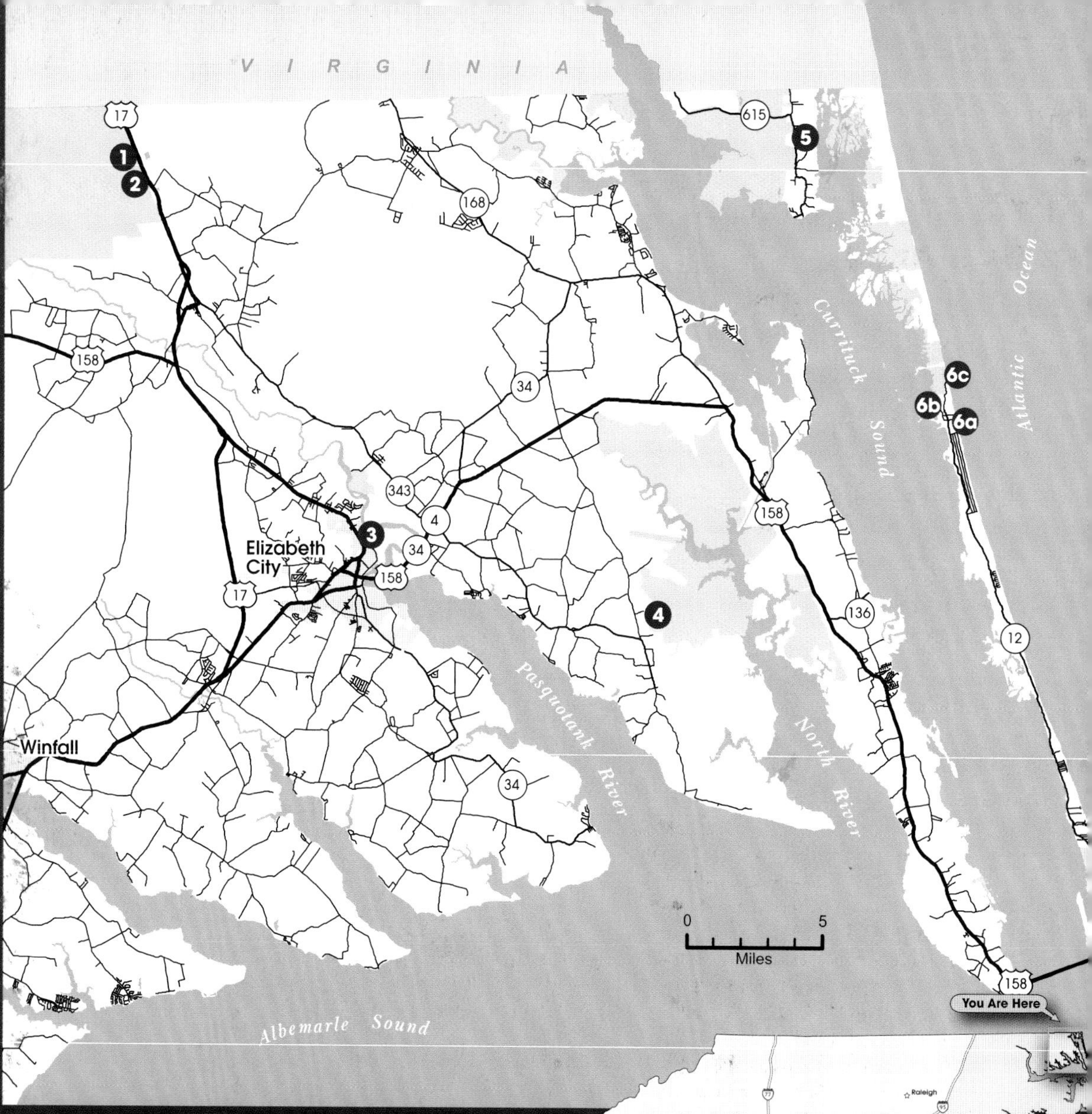

VIRGINIA

17

1
2

168

615

5

158

34

343

4

Elizabeth
City

3

34

158

158

136

6c
6b
6a

Currituck Sound

Atlantic Ocean

12

17

Winfall

Pasquotank River

North River

34

0   5
Miles

You Are Here

158

Albemarle Sound

Raleigh

Northeast Group

1 Dismal Swamp State Natural Area

2 Dismal Swamp Canal Trail

3 Regional Fitness Trail

4 North River Game Land - Harrison Tract

5 Mackay Island National Wildlife Refuge

6a Outer Banks Center for Wildlife Education

6b Currituck Banks National Estuarine
Research Reserve

6c Currituck National Wildlife Refuge

1

Dismal Swamp State Natural Area

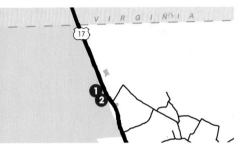

Site Information:
Owner: NC State Parks
2294 US 17 North, South Mills, NC 27976
Camden County
252-771-6593
www.ncsparks.net

About the Site:

The Dismal Swamp State Natural Area is a 14,344 acre natural area, managed for the public to enjoy. Within the Natural Area are more than 20 miles of maintained logging roads; several boardwalks are under construction (as of 2006). The Natural Area offers a wide array of recreational opportunities such as butterfly watching, birding, hiking, canoeing and kayaking. The 300 foot boardwalk located behind the visitor center is an excellent place to get a taste of the birds that make the Dismal Swamp their home. Canal Road, which runs parallel to the Dismal Swamp Canal, is another good location. If you are more adventurous, travel down the Kim Saunders Trail (approximately 5 miles in length) to one of the few remaining Atlantic White Cedar stands left in the east. Over 100 species of birds have been identified by park staff in the last year.

Species of Interest: Great Crested Flycatcher, Prothonotary Warbler, Hooded Warbler, Summer Tanager, Indigo Bunting

Habitats: floodplain forest, canal, wetland forest

Special Features/Concerns: This site is under development as of 2006 and is difficult to access during the construction of the new visitor center. Completion of the site is scheduled for Summer/Fall 2007. Please contact the park for information on construction progress.

Access & Parking: Enter the Dismal Swamp Canal Welcome Center parking area for cars. The Natural Area's parking lot is located through the south gate just past the Welcome Center. Enter the Natural Area at the bridge (foot/bike traffic only). Call ahead to inquire about hours of operation.

Directions: From the village of South Mills, take the US Hwy 17 Bypass north for 5 miles to the entrance of the Dismal Swamp State Natural Area and Dismal Swamp Canal Welcome Center. The Natural Area is 3 miles south of the Virginia/North Carolina border and 18 miles north of Elizabeth City, NC.

Coordinates: N 36°30'25" W 76°21'17"
DeLorme (NC Gazetteer) Page: 25

© NC State Parks

Birders along the trail

Northeast Group

13

© Jeff Le

Dismal Swamp Canal Trail

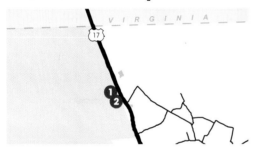

Site Information:

Owner: NC Department of Transportation
and Dismal Swamp Canal Welcome Center
2356 US 17 North, South Mills, NC 27976
Camden County
877-771-8333
www.dismalswamp.com

About the Site:

Located in Camden County on scenic US 17 just three miles south of the Virginia/North Carolina border, the Dismal Swamp Canal Welcome Center sits on the banks of the Dismal Swamp Canal, part of the Atlantic Intracoastal Waterway. Starting at the Welcome Center, the Dismal Swamp Canal Trail is a 10 foot wide, hard-surfaced trail that winds its way between US 17 and the historic Dismal Swamp Canal for approximately 3 miles. It then becomes a highway extension of NC 343 and Mullen Road to the village of South Mills, an additional 1.5 miles. Benches and picnic tables are available, and mile markers line the path. Bird feeders and birdhouses can be found along the trail. Trail bikes are available at the Welcome Center for visitors to enjoy at no charge - bikes are secured by a Driver's License.

Species of Interest: Great Crested Flycatcher, Prothonotary Warbler, Hooded Warbler, Summer Tanager, Indigo Bunting

Habitats: floodplain forest, canal, wetland forest

Access & Parking: Ample parking is available in the Welcome Center lot. Welcome Center hours of operation are November - May: 9am to 5pm, Tuesday - Saturday; June - October: 9am to 5pm, daily.

Directions: From the village of South Mills, take US Hwy 17 Bypass north for 5 miles to the entrance of the Welcome Center. The Center is 3 miles south of the VA/NC border and 18 miles north of Elizabeth City, NC.

Coordinates: N 36°30'25" W 76°21'17"
DeLorme (NC Gazetteer) Page: 25

3

Regional Fitness Trail ♿ 🚶 🚻

Site Information:
Contact: College of the Albemarle and Albemarle Hospital
1208 North Road Street, Elizabeth City, NC 27906
Pasquotank County
252-335-0821 x 2211

About the Site:
As you drive into this site, watch for the entrance to the 0.5 mile long boardwalk on the left side of the street by the campus buildings, identified as the College of the Albemarle Fenwick-Hollowell Wetlands Trail. From this entrance, the boardwalk takes you through a wet area with uprooted trees and thick vegetation that provides suitable habitat for cardinals, flycatchers, vireos and other songbirds. A short distance later, you emerge onto a canal that leads to the wide expanse of the Pasquotank River. Along the canal, there are good viewing opportunities for both resident and migrating songbirds. Watch for Green Heron and other wading birds at the water's edge. As the trail reaches the Pasquotank River, search the cypress trees hanging with Spanish moss for additional species. Watch for a beaver dam where the canal meets the river. Benches and gazebos along the river provide opportunities to sit quietly, listen and observe. The gazebos are home to Barn Swallow during the summer. Along the river a stand of phragmites provides habitat and cover that can be searched for additional species.

© Phil Rhyne

Snowy Egret

Species of Interest: Prothonotary Warbler, wading birds

Habitats: pine/hardwood forest, isolated wetlands, marsh, river

Access & Parking: From the entrance, drive to the back of the college and park in the overflow parking area away from the buildings. Access the boardwalk where the woods and swamp border the college to the north. Open daily during daylight hours. Restrooms are available at the college.

Directions: From the intersection of US 17 and US 158 in Elizabeth City, travel approximately 1 mile north to the college entrance on the east side of the road, just past the Albemarle Hospital.

Coordinates: N 36°19'32" W 76°13'05"
DeLorme (NC Gazetteer) Page: 26

Northeast Group

North River Game Land

Site Information:
Owner: NC Wildlife Resources Commission
Indian Island Road, off of Sassafras Lane,
south of Shiloh, NC
Camden County
252-482-7701
www.ncwildlife.org

About the Site:
The one primary dirt road through the middle of the North River Game Land provides good birding opportunities. If you have the energy to make it 3 miles, you will find a 55 acre waterfowl impoundment at the end of the road and will have chances to see wading birds, shorebirds and wintering waterfowl. Even if you don't make it the full distance, you will pass through both upland and swamp forest habitats along the way, with opportunities to see and hear birds typical of these habitat types. Wood Duck are present year-round, along with Wood Thrush, Prothonotary, Swainson's and Hooded Warblers during the summer. Watch and listen for Brown-headed Nuthatch and Indigo Bunting in open pine woodlands.

Species of Interest: Brown-headed Nuthatch, Swainson's Warbler, Hooded Warbler, Indigo Bunting, wintering waterfowl

Habitats: pine/hardwood forest, isolated wetlands, managed waterfowl impoundment, early successional

Special Concern: Hunting is allowed on Game Lands during certain times of year. Birders should be aware of current hunting regulations and seasons and take adequate safety precautions during those times. For more on hunting precautions, see the hunting season information at the beginning of this guide.

Access & Parking: The gate to North River Game Land is closed from March 1 - September 1, but foot travel is allowed. Limited parking is located near the gate, approximately 0.25 miles along Indian Island Road. Please do not block the gate when parking. If the gate is open, birding by vehicle is allowed, but 4-wheel drive is suggested. It is highly recommended that visitors request a current Game Lands Map Book from the NC Wildlife Resources Commission before visiting.

Directions: From Shiloh, take NC 343 south for approximately 2.5 miles. Turn left on Sandy Hook Road. Go 0.1 miles and turn right on Sassafras Lane. After traveling 0.4 miles down Sassafras Lane, turn left on the gravel road that heads toward the treeline - this is Indian Island Road, though there is no sign marking the road. The Game Land boundary begins at the orange gate on Indian Island Road.

Coordinates: N 36° 16'12" W 76° 01'45"
DeLorme (NC Gazetteer) Page: 26

© Harry Sell

Indigo Buntin

16

Cattle Egret

5

Mackay Island National Wildlife Refuge

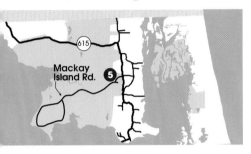

Mackay Island Rd. **5**

615

Site Information:
Owner: US Fish and Wildlife Service
NC 615, Knotts Island, NC 27950
Currituck County
252-429-3100
www.fws.gov/mackayisland/index.html

About the Site:
Take Mackay Island Road for 2 miles to the parking area for the Mackay Island Trail (3.8 miles roundtrip) or the Live Oak Point Trail (6.5 miles roundtrip) around East, Middle and West Pools. Explore the 0.3 mile Great Marsh Trail loop along NC 615 and stop at the Kuralt Trail Overlook at Barleys Bay. During fall and winter, watch for a variety of waterfowl, including Snow Goose, Green-winged and Blue-winged Teal, Northern Pintail, Northern Shoveler, Gadwall and American Wigeon. During warmer months, watch and listen for Marsh Wren, rails, and wading birds. An active Wood Duck breeding population is present on the refuge. There is visual access to Currituck Sound and the Kitchin Impoundment at the Joseph P. Knapp Visitor Contact Station. Wildlife interpretive displays and literature can be found there, as well as at the Kuralt Trail Overlook and the Mackay Island Road entrance.

Species of Interest: Snow Goose, Bald Eagle, rails, wading birds, wintering waterfowl

Habitats: managed waterfowl impoundments, salt marsh, wetland forest, isolated wetlands

Special Concern: Hunting is allowed on refuges during certain times of year. Birders should be aware of current hunting regulations and seasons and take adequate safety precautions during those times. For more on hunting season safety precautions, see the hunting season information at the beginning of this guide.

Access & Parking: There are 3 access roads through the refuge: Mackay Island Road, the Marsh Causeway, and the road to the Joseph P. Knapp Visitor Contact Station. To reach East, Middle , and West Pools, travel Mackay Island Road for 2 miles to the parking area. Walking trails are found along NC 615 and around East, Middle and West Pool. There is a wildlife observation platform and parking lot on the north side of NC 615 on Barleys Bay. The refuge is open daily during daylight hours, with the exception of the area near the refuge office, which is open from 7:30am to 4pm, Monday - Friday. Visitors are strongly encouraged to stop at refuge headquarters to pick up a refuge brochure, map and bird list.

Directions: Traveling from the south, the free Currituck Sound ferry is available with travel between Currituck, NC (via NC 168) and Knotts Island, NC. Road access to the refuge via Virginia is from NC 615. The refuge office is 1 mile south of Virginia Beach, VA, just over the North Carolina border on NC 615.

Coordinates: N 36°31'40" W 75°59'25"
DeLorme (NC Gazetteer) Page: 26

Northeast Group

Outer Banks Center for Wildlife Education

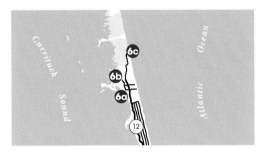

Boardwalk Birding

Site Information:
Owner: NC Wildlife Resources Commission
1160 Village Lane, Corolla, NC 27927
Currituck County
252-453-0221
www.ncwildlife.org

About the Site:

The grounds surrounding the Outer Banks Center for Wildlife Education provide visitors with quality birding opportunities. A 0.25 mile boardwalk leads through maritime forest and marsh habitats and extends into Currituck Sound. Heritage Park also provides birding opportunities with its open habitat, canal, pond, shoreline and live oaks. In the colder months, waterfowl abound in the sound. In the warmer months, look for wading birds, terns, and nesting songbirds. Typically, there are multiple Osprey nests in the vicinity each summer. Migrating and wintering warblers can easily be spotted from fall through spring. Stop in the Center to learn about the natural and cultural history of Currituck Sound and the Outer Banks.

Species of Interest: Least Tern, Black Skimmer, wading birds, wintering waterfowl

Habitats: maritime forest and shrub, salt marsh

Special Features: The Currituck Beach Lighthouse and the Whalehead Club are other attractions within walking distance of the Outer Banks Center for Wildlife Education.

Access & Parking: Ample parking is available in the Education Center lot. Open daily, 10am to 6pm, April - October; 9am to 5pm, November - March.

Directions: Take NC 12 north from Duck to Corolla. The Education Center is located on the sound side of the road in Currituck Heritage Park, between the Whalehead Club and the Currituck Beach Lighthouse.

Coordinates: N 36°22'29" W 75°49'50"
DeLorme (NC Gazetteer) Page: 26

© Mark Buckler   Green Heron

© Mark Buckler

Marsh along Currituck Sound

6b

Currituck Banks National Estuarine Research Reserve

♿ 🚶 ❓ 🏞

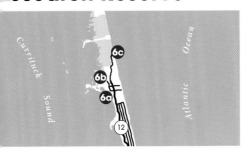

Site Information:
Owner: NC Coastal Reserve
1 mile north of Corolla, NC, at the end of NC 12
Currituck County
252-261-8891
www.nccoastalreserve.net

About the Site:

The Currituck Banks National Estuarine Research Reserve site lies in the northeastern corner of North Carolina, 10 miles south of the Virginia border and a mile north of the village of Corolla. Bounded by Currituck Sound and the Atlantic Ocean, the site encompasses 954 acres. The Nature Conservancy and the US Fish and Wildlife Service own neighboring tracts. The best way to access the site is along a 0.3 mile boardwalk that begins at the parking lot and leads to a view of Currituck Sound; signs along the way give information about the site. A 0.75 mile primitive trail departs from the boardwalk and heads north through maritime forest, also ending at Currituck Sound. Within the forest, listen for Pine Warbler, Blue-gray Gnatcatcher, Indigo Bunting, and Caro-

lina Wren. Near the sound, watch for waterfowl and shorebirds during fall and winter. During warmer months, listen for Common Yellowthroat, and watch for Osprey, Least Tern, Black Skimmer and wading birds. During spring, the shrub thickets hold migrating songbirds.

Species of Interest: Least Tern, Black Skimmer, Indigo Bunting, wintering waterfowl, wading birds, migrating songbirds

Habitats: maritime forest and shrub, brackish marsh

Special Concern: Hunting is allowed on coastal reserves during certain times of year. Birders should be aware of current hunting regulations and seasons and take adequate safety precautions during those times. For more on hunting season safety precautions, see the hunting season information at the beginning of this guide.

Access & Parking: Main access to the site is by boardwalk and trail. Both are reached from the parking area. Open daily during daylight hours.

Directions: Drive north on US 12, 0.75 miles past the Currituck Beach Lighthouse. At a sharp right turn in the road, drive straight ahead into the parking area, which is marked with a sign.

Coordinates: N 36°23'20" W 75°49'50"
DeLorme (NC Gazetteer) Page: 26

Northeast Group

© NC National Estuarine Research Reserve

Curriituck National Wildlife Refuge

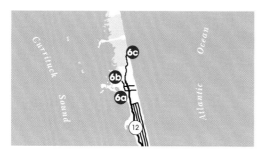

Site Information:
Owner: US Fish and Wildlife Service
Just north of Corolla, NC, beyond the end of
NC 12
Currituck County
252-429-3100
www.fws.gov/mackayisland/currituck/

About the Site:

Currituck National Wildlife Refuge is located
north of Corolla, NC. The refuge is comprised
of 5 distinct tracts, totalling 3,213 acres. The
380 acre Monkey Island tract is the most
easily accessed portion of the refuge, located
just north of the end of NC 12, beyond tracts
owned by the NC National Estuarine Research Reserve and The Nature Conservancy.
This tract includes a mix of beach, dune and
maritime thicket habitats. The ocean side
along this stretch of the barrier island is best
birded from winter to early spring. Watch for
Northern Gannet, Common and Red-throated
Loon, Horned Grebe, and mergansers. During
spring migration, scan the shrubs for migrating songbirds and watch for shorebirds feeding
in the surf zone. During the summer months,
be aware of the possibility of nesting Piping
Plover and Least Tern colonies. Do not disturb
nesting birds.

Black-bellied Plover

Species of Interest: Red-throated Loon,
Horned Grebe, Piping Plover, Least Tern,
wintering waterfowl

Habitats: maritime forest and shrub, salt
marsh, beach and dune

Special Concern: Foot traffic may be limited during the spring and summer months
to protect beach-nesting birds. Interpretive
materials must be picked up at the Mackay
Island National Wildlife Refuge office. Hunting is allowed on refuges during certain
times of year. Birders should be aware of
current hunting regulations and seasons
and take adequate safety precautions during those times. For more on hunting season
safety precautions, see the hunting season
information at the beginning of this guide.

Access & Parking: The refuge has no roads,
trails or parking lots, but is open to foot traffic or vehicle use (4-wheel drive necessary).
The refuge is open daily during daylight
hours. There are 5 main refuge tracts, all
of which can be accessed by boat across
Currituck Sound, but only some of which
can be accessed from Currituck Banks. The
Monkey Island and Swan Island tracts can
be accessed by walking or driving north
along the beach at the end of the paved
road. The paved road (NC 12) ends approximately 0.75 miles south of the Monkey
Island tract and about 4.3 miles south of the
Swan Island tract. From the parking area,
use the nearby North Beach access ramp to
get to the beach and then head north.

Directions: To access the Monkey Island or
Swan Island tracts, drive north on NC 12, 1
mile past the Currituck Beach Lighthouse.
At a sharp right turn in the road, drive
straight ahead into the Currituck Banks National Estuarine Research Reserve parking
area (foot traffic access) or use the North
Beach access ramp to drive north along
the beach (4-wheel drive required). All of
the refuge tracts are also accessible by
small boat across Currituck Sound.

Coordinates: N 36°23'20" W 75°49'50"
DeLorme (NC Gazetteer) Page: 26

© Mark Buckler

Sunset over Currituck Sound

Tricolored Heron

While You're In the Area

Currituck Beach Lighthouse
Currituck Heritage Park
Corolla, NC 27927
252-453-8152
www.currituckbeachlight.com

Currituck – Knotts Island Ferry
NC Department of Transportation, Ferry Division
252-232-2683
www.ncdot.org/transit/ferry

Great Dismal Swamp National Wildlife Refuge
US Fish and Wildlife Service
3100 Desert Road
Suffolk, VA 23434
757-986-3705
www.fws.gov/northeast/greatdismalswamp

(continues)

Great Blue Heron

Northeast Group

Historic Albemarle Tour, Inc.
NC Heritage Trail
PO Box 1604
Washington, NC 27889
800-734-1117
www.historicnenc.com

HomegrownHandmade
Art Roads and Farm Trails of North Carolina
www.homegrownhandmade.com

Museum of the Albemarle
501 S. Water Street
Elizabeth City, NC 27909
252-335-1453
www.museumofthealbemarle.com

The Whalehead Club
Currituck Heritage Park
Corolla, NC 27927
252-453-9040
www.whaleheadclub.com

Welcome to the
Tri-County Group

Bordered by the Albemarle Sound to the south, the Tri-county Group is rich with blackwater streams, as well as historic millponds, towns and communities. With small tributaries feeding into the broad rivers, paddling opportunities abound for quiet, remote birding at streamside and by ear. Boardwalks along creeks and rivers enhance up-close observation of these wetland communities and local bed and breakfasts provide attractive lodging choices.

You Are Here

77

☆ Raleigh

95

Tri-County Group

© NC State Parks

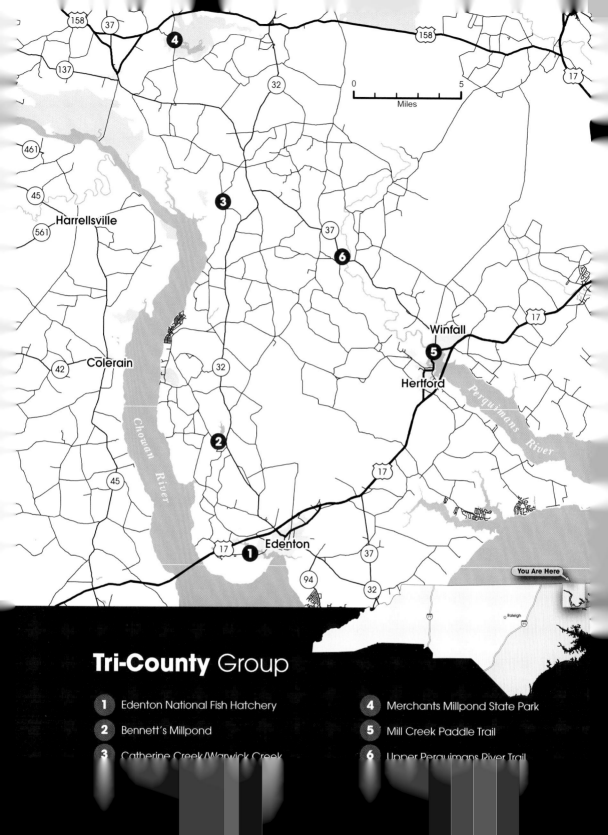

Tri-County Group

1. Edenton National Fish Hatchery
2. Bennett's Millpond
3. Catherine Creek/Warwick Creek
4. Merchants Millpond State Park
5. Mill Creek Paddle Trail
6. Upper Perquimans River Trail

You Are Here

Edenton National Fish Hatchery

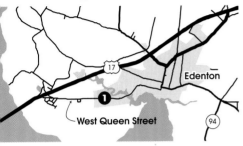

Site Information:
Owner: US Fish and Wildlife Service
1102 West Queen Street (US 17 Business),
Edenton, NC 27932
Chowan County
252-482-4118
www.fws.gov/edenton/

About the Site:
Egrets, herons and cormorants alike know they can find a quick gourmet meal of striped bass and American shad at the Edenton Fish Hatchery. During harvest season from May to mid-December you might witness a feeding frenzy of cormorants and wading birds as fish are removed from the grow-out ponds to restock local rivers. As individual ponds are drawn down to congregate the fish, pond edges attract shorebirds, while others take advantage of the dense fish population. After parking and a quick visit to the aquarium, walk thru the gate behind the building to the gravel road that bisects the hatchery. As you walk through the hatchery toward the river, meander around the 36 ponds on either side of the road to search for Osprey, waterfowl and shorebirds. Continue to the back of the hatchery where you'll see a short boardwalk that ends with a viewing platform on scenic Pembroke Creek, where migrating songbirds return to nest. The boardwalk crosses a short expanse of floodplain forest, where you might see a Prothonotary Warbler, or hear an Acadian Flycatcher or Yellow-billed Cuckoo in the spring and summer.

Osprey in flight

Species of Interest: Bald Eagle, Prothonotary Warbler, shorebirds, wading birds, wintering waterfowl

Habitats: floodplain forest, hatchery ponds, creek

Special Features: The annual Fishing Rodeo and Hatchery Open House take place in June. Small and large group hatchery tours can be arranged in advance. The hatchery is most active during April and May as American shad eggs are developing in glass hatching jars. Striped bass are harvested in June and November for stocking rivers.

Access & Parking: The hatchery is open year round from 7am to 3:30pm, Monday - Friday, as well as Saturday and Sunday from April to mid-December.

Directions: From the intersection of US 17 and US 17 Business west of Edenton (Exit 224), take US 17 Business (West Queen Street) toward Edenton. Travel 1.7 miles to the hatchery entrance on the north side of the road. The entrance is marked with a brick sign.

Coordinates: N 36°03′25″ W 76°38′13″
DeLorme (NC Gazetteer) Page: 47

Tri-County Group

2

Bennett's Millpond ⛴ ⛺ 🚶 ⛲ 🔭

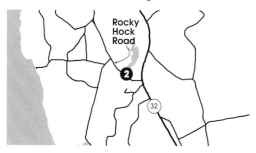

Cypress at Bennett's Millpond

Site Information:

Contact: Edenton-Chowan Parks and Recreation Department
Rocky Hock Road, west of NC 32 and north of Edenton, NC
Chowan County
252-482-8595
www.ncsu.edu/paddletrails

About the Site:

Bennett's Millpond is the perfect site for a half-day paddle to explore its upper reaches and experience the charm of a traditional southern millpond, or walk along the boardwalk and trail. Cypress trees laden with Spanish moss are spread throughout the pond and along the edges. In denser edges of cypress, mixed hardwood and pine, migrating and resident songbirds entertain with their songs and calls. In the spring and early summer, watch and listen for Northern Parula, Prothonotary Warbler, Hooded Warbler, and Summer Tanager. In winter, watch for Hooded Mergansers. The center of the pond caters to larger birds that wing their way from tree to tree as you paddle. Summering Anhinga perched with wings spread in the treetops raise the possibility of nesting. Meanwhile, nestlings from the Great Blue Heron rookery at the back of the pond create an eerie primordial atmosphere with their guttural begging sounds. Bennett's Millpond has considerable underwater vegetation in the more shallow edges to catch paddles but it only makes you wonder what other creatures call the millpond home. With no directional markers, use the cypress trees and other points for reference to avoid becoming disoriented.

Species of Interest: Hooded Merganser, Anhinga, Prothonotary Warbler, Hooded Warbler, Summer Tanager, wading birds

Habitats: floodplain forest, millpond

Special Features & Concerns: Bennett's Millpond is part of the North Carolina Coastal Plain Paddle Trails System and connects with the Rockyhock Creek section of the paddle trail. From the dam at Bennett's Millpond you can paddle several miles upstream where it becomes a small stream supplying the millpond. The millpond can be disorienting so pay special attention to the directions paddled. Hunting is allowed on private land surrounding the millpond.

Access & Parking: The access road into the site is gravel. The site has a concrete boat launch and dock near the dam - use caution! Parking is available at the launch area. The site is open daily during daylight hours. Boardwalks and trails can be accessed from the parking area. Primitive camping is allowed on-site.

Directions: From the intersection of US 17 and NC 32 in Edenton, take NC 32 north for 5.8 miles. Turn west on Rocky Hock Road. The entrance to Bennett's Millpond is 0.2 miles on the right.

Coordinates: N 36°08'20" W 76°39'55"
DeLorme (NC Gazetteer) Page: 25

③ Catherine Creek/Warwick Creek Paddle Trail 🚶 🚣 ⛺

Cannon Ferry Rd. ③ Welch Rd.

Chowan River

32

Red-shouldered Hawk

Site Information:
Contact: Edenton-Chowan Parks and Recreation Department
Warwick Creek put-in at Cannon Ferry Road (SR 1232) bridge, north of Edenton, NC
Chowan County
252-482-8595
www.ncsu.edu/paddletrails

About the Site:

This trail begins in the narrows of Warwick Creek and takes the paddler downstream through scenic hardwood swamps and banks covered with low vegetation. As with most birding trips by canoe or kayak, the species list is dependent on keen ears but you might be surprised to hear Northern Bobwhite calling from a nearby farm field hidden by the trees. Red-shouldered Hawks draw attention overhead and a variety of migrating songbirds call from the shore. Listen for a variety of flycatchers and vireos, Prothonotary Warbler and possibly the elusive Swainson's Warbler. Warwick Creek continues to widen from the put-in and becomes quite broad at the confluence with the Troutman Creek tributary where it becomes Catherine Creek. From this point, it is an easy return paddle to the put-in for about a 2-3 hour round trip. If continuing downstream, hug the shoreline for birding by ear. Approaching the Chowan River, islands of cypress trees full of Spanish moss appear. Continue downstream on the Chowan River to the Wildlife Resource Commission boat access ramp for a 3-5 hour trip. In windy conditions, the wide expanses of the creek and river can make paddling difficult.

Species of Interest: Great Crested Flycatcher, Prothonotary Warbler, Swainson's Warbler, raptors, wading birds

Habitats: floodplain forest, creek

Special Concerns: This site is accessible only by boat. The Catherine Creek/Warwick Creek Paddle Trail is part of the North Carolina Coastal Plain Paddle Trails System. The trail from the put-in to the Troutman Creek tributary is suitable for an out-and-back paddle trip. The lower portion of the trail is in open water, which can be challenging on windy days.

Access & Parking: Parking for a few vehicles is available at the put-in area. Paddlers are encouraged to leave their vehicles at the NC Wildlife Resources Commission ramp on the Chowan River for take-out. Holladay's Island, in the middle of the Chowan River, offers additional paddling opportunities and 5 overnight camping platforms. Paddling this area can be difficult in windy conditions. Paddlers must call ahead to reserve these platforms.

Directions: From the intersection of US 17 and NC 32 in Edenton, take NC 32 north for about 15 miles to Cannon Ferry Road (SR 1232). Turn west on Cannon Ferry Road. In 0.9 miles, the road passes by the NC Wildlife Resources Commission boat ramp and the Chowan River. Continue on for 3.5 miles to the paddle trail put-in, at the Warwick Creek bridge.

Coordinates: N 36°18'50" W 76°39'24"
DeLorme (NC Gazetteer) Page: 25

Tri-County Group

27

A view of Merchants Millpond

Merchants Millpond State Park

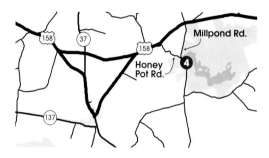

Millpond Rd.

Honey Pot Rd.

Tri-County Group

nine miles of trails that pass through the park. The best way to explore Merchants Millpond, however, is by canoeing across the park's shallow waters. Marked canoe trails lead from the boat ramp to canoe campsites. Venture out of the millpond and take slow-moving, dark-water Bennetts Creek through Lassiter Swamp, among mistletoe, hanging Spanish moss and ancient cypress trees.

Site Information:
Owner: NC State Parks
71 US 158 East, Gatesville, NC 27938
Gates County
252-357-1191
www.ncsparks.net

About the Site:
The 760-acre millpond that is the park's focus is more than 190 years old. Towering bald cypress and tupelo gum trees, displaying growths of Spanish moss and resurrection ferns, shade the pond's dark, acidic waters. More than 200 species of birds have been recorded in the park. Watch and listen for a variety of warblers, including Northern Parula, Prothonotary and Yellow-throated Warbler. In winter, a variety of waterfowl stop by on their journey south. Visitors may catch a glimpse of a Hooded Merganser, Wood Duck, Bald Eagle, Pileated Woodpecker, Barred Owl, or a Red-shouldered Hawk on their visit. Trek on any of the

©Jeff Lewis

Barred Owl

Species of Interest: Hooded Merganser, Bald Eagle, Whip-poor-will, Prothonotary Warbler

Habitats: floodplain forest, millpond

Special Concerns: Pay close attention if exploring the park by canoe or kayak. It is easy to become disoriented in the swamp forest.

Access & Parking: Parking is available at the canoe access area on Millpond Road. The park is open from 8am to 6pm, November - February; 8am to 7pm, March and October; 8am to 8pm, April, May, and September; 8am to 9pm, June - August. Canoe rentals available. A boat ramp and pier near the parking area offer access to the water.

Directions: From Gatesville, take US 158 East for 5 miles. Turn south on Millpond Road (SR 1403) and follow signs to the parking and canoe access area.

Coordinates: N 36°25'51" W 76°41'53"
DeLorme (NC Gazetteer) Page: 24

28

Mill Creek Paddle Trail

Site Information:
Contact: Town of Hertford
Put-in at Larry's Drive-In, on US 17 Business,
0.4 miles northeast of Hertford, NC
Perquimans County
252-426-1425
www.ncsu.edu/paddletrails

About the Site:

Mill Creek is described by some as the "quintessential southern swamp" but that is not immediately obvious from the put-in. To reach the creek, paddle out the short canal to the broad expanse of the Perquimans River then to the left (east) to hug the shoreline where cypress trees laden with Spanish moss provide shelter. Watch for an Osprey at the nest in the stand of cypress trees across the river as you continue toward the entrance of Mill Creek. Pass under the bridge where the creek will narrow and birding by ear becomes an asset to locate the migrating songbirds that inhabit the area in spring and summer. Listen for a variety of flycatchers, vireos, and warblers. Barred Owl and Red-shouldered Hawk may make their presence known along with other year-round residents. The banks of Mill Creek are lined with floodplain forest trees, so the understory is relatively open, allowing deeper views into the woods. After passing under the second bridge, bear to the right to enter the wetland forest that provides dense cover and a high canopy where you might hear birds and see deer and other critters near the water. The slow-moving Mill Creek offers the perfect opportunity for an out-and-back paddle.

Species of Interest: Great Crested Flycatcher, Prothonotary Warbler, raptors, wading birds

Habitats: floodplain forest, creek

Special Concerns: Southerly winds may create some chop on the Perquimans River before reaching the entrance to Mill Creek.

Access & Parking: This site is accessible only by boat. The boat launch consists of a bulkhead and a wooden boat ramp, which can be slippery - use caution! Parking is available at the launch site. Park away from the building and do not block driveways.

Directions: From Hertford, take US 17 Business northeast. Cross the Perquimans River and in 0.5 miles, turn south into Larry's Drive-In parking lot. The launch site is at the back of the parking lot.

Coordinates: N 36°11'58" W 76°27'46"
DeLorme (NC Gazetteer) Page: 25

Prothonotary Warbler

Tri-County Group

29

Upper Perquimans River Paddle Trail

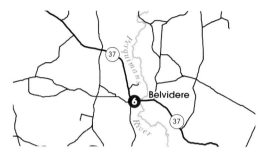

Site Information:

Contact: Town of Hertford
Put-in at NC 37 Perquimans River bridge
near Belvidere, NC
Perquimans County
252-426-1425
www.ncsu.edu/paddletrails

About the Site:

Most rivers don't provide easy out-and-back paddles but the upper portion of the narrow, gently flowing Perquimans River does just that. At rivers edge, shrubs and vines line the bank while the canopy of bald cypress and other trees provide shade for comfortable paddling conditions. With low vegetation extending over the water, migrating songbirds abound and can easily be seen flitting across the river in early spring. Later in the season, nesting locations might be visible and birding by ear will allow you to identify Great Crested Flycatcher, Prothonotary Warbler, and a variety of vireos, among others. Overhead, Red-shouldered Hawks scream for attention. For the best birding, paddle upstream under the bridge where you are likely to see Barn Swallows nesting in the summer. The bridge may create a bit of a current, but a few feet beyond the bridge the current is nearly undetectable even at high water. For those wishing to paddle only one direction, there is a take-out upstream of the put-in at Perry's Creek Road that can be reached in 3-4 hours.

Species of Interest: Great Crested Flycatcher, Prothonotary Warbler, raptors, wading birds

Habitats: floodplain forest, river

Special Feature: The Upper Perquimans River Paddle Trail is part of the North Carolina Coastal Plain Paddle Trails system. The portion of the river north of the NC 37 bridge provides the best habitat for birding. The portion of the trail south of the bridge provides extensive paddling opportunities but is not recommended for serious birding.

Access & Parking: This site is accessible only by boat. The boat launch consists of a concrete boat ramp with an adjoining boardwalk. Parking is available at the launch site.

Directions: From Hertford, take US 17 Business north. Cross the Perquimans River and in 0.5 miles, turn north onto NC 37. The launch site is approximately 7.8 miles from the US 17/NC 37 intersection, at the bridge just past the town of Belvidere. The launch and parking lot are adjacent to the NC 37 bridge.

Coordinates: N 36°16'06" W 76°32'42"
DeLorme (NC Gazetteer) Page: 25

© Lena Gallitano

Kayakers on the Upper Perquimans Rive

Tri-County Group

© Walker Golder

A beautiful day at Merchants Millpond

Into the swamp

© NC State Parks

While You're In the Area

Historic Albemarle Tour, Inc.
NC Heritage Trail
PO Box 1604
Washington, NC 27889
800-734-1117
www.historicnenc.com

HomegrownHandmade
Art Roads and Farm Trails of North Carolina
www.homegrownhandmade.com

J. Robert Hendrix Park & Cannon's Ferry Heritage River Walk
331 Cannon's Ferry Road
Tyner, NC 27980
252-482-8595
www.visitedenton.com/activities.htm

(continues)

The view from a kayak

Eastern Screech-Owl

Missing Mill Park
Town of Hertford
Hertford, NC 27944
www.visitperquimans.com/content/
Attractions/intro.shtml

Newbold-White House
Harvey Point Road
Hertford, NC 27944
252-426-7567
www.newboldwhitehouse.com

Trestle House Inn
632 Soundside Road
Edenton, NC 27932
800-645-8466
www.trestlehouseinn.com

Welcome to the
I-95 Corridor Group

The I-95 Corridor is characterized by rural farmlands bisected by majestic bottomland forests that follow two major rivers, the Tar and Roanoke Rivers. Indigo Bunting, Common Yellowthroat, and Field Sparrow sing from the margins of the upland farm fields in the summer, and sparrows congregate in the same areas in the winter. The bottomland forests are rich in both plant and animal diversity and are filled with migrating songbirds in the spring and fall. A large number of waterfowl spend their winters along the rivers and in the associated wetlands.

You Are Here

77

Raleigh

95

I-95 Corridor

© Craig Ellison

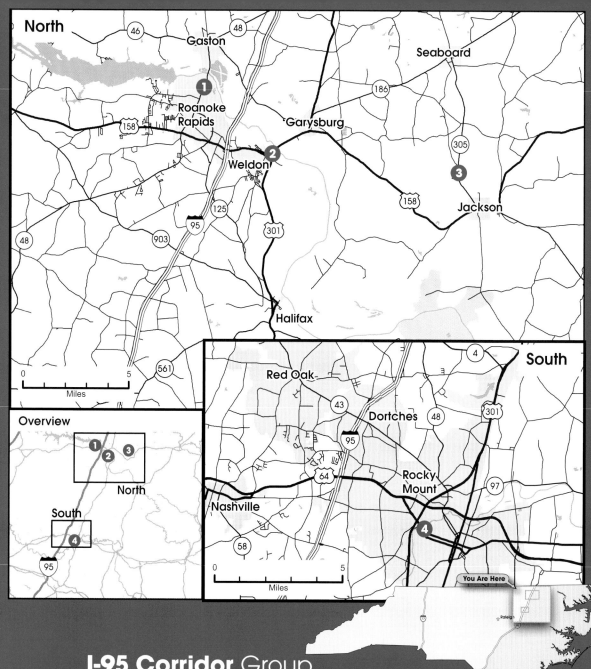

I-95 Corridor Group

1 Roanoke Canal Museum & Trail

2 Roanoke River Paddle Trail - Weldon

3 Northampton County Nature Trail

4 Tar River Trail

1

Roanoke Canal Museum and Trail

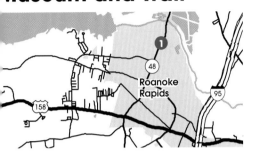

Site Information:
Owner: Roanoke Canal Museum and Trail
Roanoke Rapids to Weldon, NC. Trail Heads:
Oakwood Avenue, Roanoke Rapids, NC and
River Falls Park, Weldon, NC
Halifax County
252-537-2769
www.roanokecanal.com

About the Site:
The Roanoke Canal Museum and Trail offers public access to the upper Roanoke River, an area otherwise accessible only by boat. The canal trail is an excellent place to see birds associated with mature bottomland forest and riverine aquatic habitats. The convenient parking and well-maintained path make for easy walking and viewing of birds. There is a small population of Cerulean Warbler along the river from the Chockyotte Creek aqueduct downstream to the US 158 bridge. Bald Eagle often can be seen along the stretch from NC 48 to below Weldon, particularly during the winter months. Mississippi Kite may be seen collecting insects overhead. Breeding Swainson's Warblers are tightly packed into the canebrakes and shrubby understory along the river, especially between the aqueduct and US 158 bridge. Migrating songbirds such as Black-throated Blue and Blackpoll Warbler are common in the spring, and mature forest songbirds like Acadian Flycatcher, Yellow-throated Vireo, Hooded Warbler, Prothonotary Warbler, American Redstart, Yellow-throated Warbler, and Louisiana Waterthrush nest along the trail.

During the winter months, flocks of Cedar Waxwing move through the forest canopy, and less common species such as Red-headed Woodpecker, Brown Creeper, Winter Wren, and Fox Sparrow also can be found along the trail.

Species of Interest: Bald Eagle, Mississippi Kite, Cerulean Warbler, Swainson's Warbler

Habitats: floodplain forest, river

Special Feature: The canal trail parallels the Roanoke River, which is one of the largest rivers in the Southeast and is recognized as having outstanding ecological significance.

Access & Parking: The 7.8 mile trail can be accessed during daylight hours, year round. The Roanoke Canal Museum is open 10am to 4pm, Tuesday - Saturday. There are 4 additional access points to the trail, each with parking: Oakwood Avenue and River Road in Roanoke Rapids; and the Aqueduct and River Falls Park, off of US 158, in Weldon. Download a trail guide at www.roanokecanal.com or call the Museum to request a trail guide.

Directions: To the Roanoke Canal Museum and Trail access: Once in Roanoke Rapids, follow Roanoke Avenue (NC 48) past 1st Street. Turn left on the Jackson Street Extension immediately past a Shell Station on the left. The museum is up on the hill.

Coordinates: N 36°28'28" W 77°38'53"
DeLorme (NC Gazetteer) Page: 22

© Harry Sell

American Redstart

I-95 Corridor Group

35

②

Roanoke River Paddle Trail 🛶 🎣 ⛺ 💲 🔫 ❓ 🔭
- Weldon to US 258 Bridge

Site Information:
Contact: Roanoke River Partners
Weldon, NC to the US 258 Bridge, north of
Scotland Neck, NC.
Roanoke River Partners office: 102 North
Front Street, Hamilton, NC 27840
Halifax/Northampton County line
252-798-3920
www.roanokeriverpartners.org

About the Site:
This 30 mile section of the upper Roanoke
River flows through the most extensive bottomland hardwood forests east of the Mississippi.
During migration and the breeding season, this
area supports a huge diversity of songbirds.
Limited development along the river creates a
pristine, remote experience, with opportunities to hear specialty species such as Cerulean
Warbler and Swainson's Warbler. Also be on
the lookout for Mississippi Kite and
Bald Eagle overhead. The
Tillery Camping Platform is
located halfway down this
section of river, 15 miles
downstream of the Wel-
don put-in. Consult with
Roanoke River Partners
to determine appropri-
ate routes and access
points, depending on
time constraints and river
conditions.

Swainson's Warbler

Species of Interest: Mississippi Kite, Bald
Eagle, Cerulean Warbler, Swainson's Warbler

Habitats: floodplain forest, river

Special Concern: Hunting takes place on
lands along the Roanoke River during certain times of year. Birders should be aware
of current hunting regulations and seasons
and take adequate safety precautions during those times. For more on hunting season
safety precautions, see the hunting season
information at the beginning of this guide.

Access & Parking: Paddle or small boat
access required. Birders wishing to paddle
portions of the Roanoke River Paddle Trail
should contact Roanoke River Partners
for an official trail guide and map and for
information on current river conditions.
Reservations for overnight camping platforms (fee) must be made in advance. The
put-in along this stretch of river is at the NC
Wildlife Resources Commission boat ramp
in Weldon. The take-out is at the NC Wildlife
Resources Commission boat ramp on US
258, north of Scotland Neck.

Directions: To the put-in at Weldon: the NC
Wildlife Resources Commission boat ramp
is on the southeast side of the US 301/158
bridge over the Roanoke River, in Weldon.
To the take-out on US 258: From Weldon,
take US 301 south for 8 miles, through the
town of Halifax, to NC 561. Turn left on NC
561 and travel for 15 miles to the junction of
US 258. Turn left and take US 258 north for 1.3
miles to the NC Wildlife Resources Commission boat ramp at the Roanoke River bridge.
Roanoke River Partners can provide an
official trail guide and map.

Coordinates: N 36°25'38" W 77°35'28"
(Weldon boat ramp)
DeLorme (NC Gazetteer) Page: 22

Boardwalk on the Northampton County Nature Trail

Northampton County Nature Trail

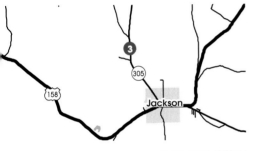

Oriole may be viewed from the boardwalk. Great Egret and other wading birds visit the wetland in the warmer months, while waterfowl may be viewed in the winter. Keep an eye out for winter sparrows under the powerline or around the wetland. The entire trail covers about 15 acres of the approximately 200-acre property and can be traversed from the parking lot to the boardwalk and back in approximately 45 minutes.

I-95 Corridor Group

Site Information:
Owner: Northampton County Cooperative Extension
9495 NC Hwy 305 North, Jackson, NC 27845
Northampton County
252-534-2711
http://northampton.ces.ncsu.edu/

Species of Interest: Eastern Kingbird, Indigo Bunting, Orchard Oriole, wading birds, winter sparrows

Habitats: floodplain forest, early successional, pond

Access & Parking: A parking lot is located on the north side of the J. W. Faison Administrative Building. The trail begins adjacent to the lot on its west side. The trail is open for daily use from 8:30am to 4:30pm. Restrooms are located in the Administrative Building, open 8:30am to 5pm, Monday - Friday.

About the Site:
The Northampton Nature Trail is a gem hidden away in the rural countryside of eastern North Carolina. Convenient parking, an improved surface walking trail, and a wooden boardwalk offer easy access and bring birders within close view of birds. Tree identification tags and other interpretive signage add to the outdoor experience. During the spring and summer months, a diversity of early-succession songbirds can be seen and heard along the trail. Nesting Eastern Kingbird and Orchard

Directions: Come into Jackson on US 158. At the stop light, turn north on NC 305. The J.W. Faison Administration Building is approximately 2 miles north, on the left.

Coordinates: N 36°24'50" W 77°26'09"
DeLorme (NC Gazetteer) Page: 23

Tar River Trail

Site Information:

Owner: City of Rocky Mount Parks & Recreation Department
Trail Heads: City Lake/Sunset Park, at Sunset Avenue and River Drive, and Martin Luther King, Jr. Park, on Leggett Road, Rocky Mount, NC
Nash County
252-972-1151
www.ci.rocky-mount.nc.us

About the Site:

The scenic paved trail meanders through 3 miles of floodplain forest bordering the Tar River. The trail offers year round birding opportunities. A diversity of breeding songbirds, including Acadian Flycatcher and Wood Thrush, can be seen in late spring and sum-

mer. Battle Park, located along the central portion of the trail, offers good chances to see these species, and other migrating and breeding songbirds. The length of trail between Sunset Park and Battle Park intersects a diversity of habitats and should provide excellent birding in the fall and winter. Visitors to the trail in March and April might bring a fishing rod and try their hand at catching the hickory and American shad that run the Tar River below the Battle Park Dam (current NC fishing license required).

Species of Interest: Acadian Flycatcher, Brown Creeper, Winter Wren, migrating songbirds, wintering waterfowl

Habitats: floodplain forest, river

Special Features: Additional unique features along the trail include Falls of the Tar River at the Battle Park dam, rocky outcroppings located at Battle Park, the longest laminated wooden bridge in the United States, and an elevated wooden boardwalk.

Access & Parking: The 3.1 mile trail can be accessed during daylight hours, year round. The start of the trail is at Martin Luther King, Jr. Park. Parking also is available at Battle Park, Stith-Talbert Park, and Sunset Park, the terminus of the Trail. Seasonal concessions are available at Sunset Park. Call Rocky Mount Parks & Recreation to request a trail map or download a trail map from www.ci.rocky-mount.nc.us.

Directions: To the Sunset Park access area: take US 64 to the Peachtree/Benvenue Street Exit. Turn south on Peachtree Street, then right on River Drive and right into Sunset Park.

Coordinates: N 35°57'06" W 77°49'07"
DeLorme (NC Gazetteer) Page: 42

Tar River Trail

I-95 Corridor Group

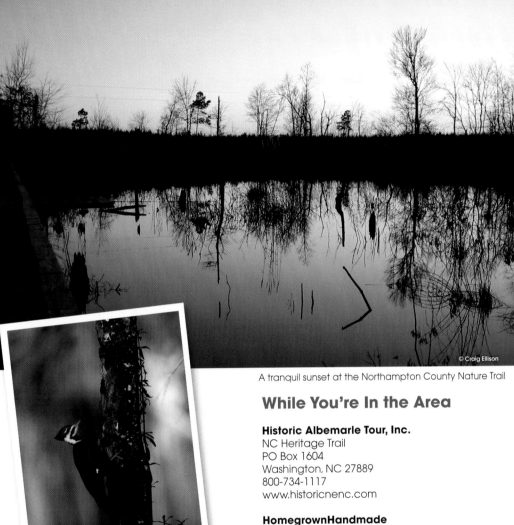

© Craig Ellison

A tranquil sunset at the Northampton County Nature Trail

© Walker Golder

Pileated Woodpecker

While You're In the Area

Historic Albemarle Tour, Inc.
NC Heritage Trail
PO Box 1604
Washington, NC 27889
800-734-1117
www.historicnenc.com

HomegrownHandmade
Art Roads and Farm Trails of North Carolina
www.homegrownhandmade.com

Roanoke Canal Museum
15 Jackson Street Extension
Roanoke Rapids, NC 27870
252-537-2769
www.roanokecanal.com

(continues)

© Harry Sell

Mississippi Kite

Roanoke River Paddle Trail
Roanoke River Partners
102 North Front Street
Hamilton, NC 27840
252-792-3790
www.roanokeriverpartners.org

Sylvan Heights Waterfowl Park & Eco-Center
4963 Hwy 258
Scotland Neck, NC 27874
252-826-3186
http://shwpark.com/

Wilson Botanical Gardens
1806 S.W. Goldsboro Street
Wilson, NC 27893
252-237-0113
www.wilson-co.com/arboretum.html

Welcome to the
Roanoke Group

The Roanoke River region is dominated by wetlands that include some of the finest examples of bottomland forest remaining in the mid-Atlantic seaboard. This complex mosaic of forest types and river networks is an incredibly valuable habitat for songbirds, raptors, waterfowl, and other birds during all seasons. Some of the breeding birds of highest conservation concern in the southeast are commonly found in this area, including the Bald Eagle, Cerulean Warbler, Prothonotary Warbler, Swainson's Warbler, and Hooded Warbler. During spring migration alone, the diversity and abundance of migrating songbirds is a breathtaking reward for birders.

You Are Here

Raleigh

© Walker Golder

Roanoke Group

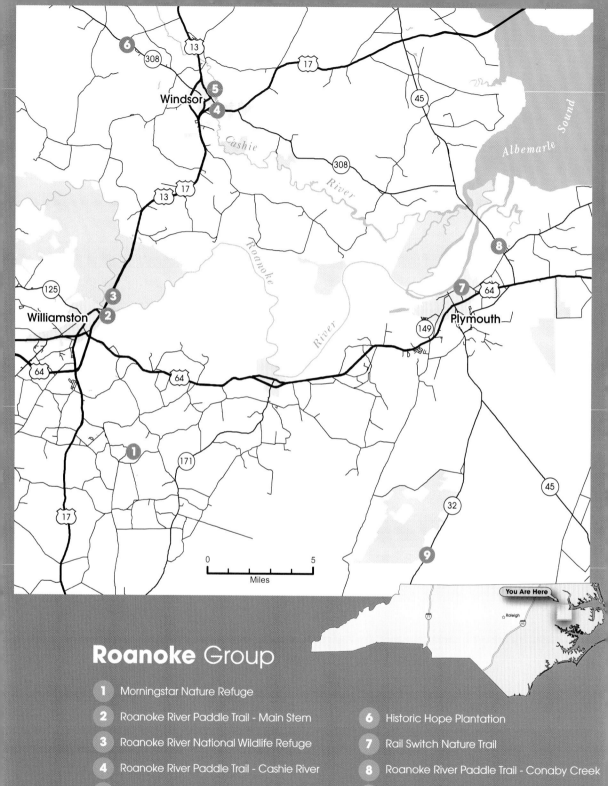

Roanoke Group

1 Morningstar Nature Refuge

2 Roanoke River Paddle Trail - Main Stem

3 Roanoke River National Wildlife Refuge

4 Roanoke River Paddle Trail - Cashie River

5 Cashie Wetlands Walk

6 Historic Hope Plantation

7 Rail Switch Nature Trail

8 Roanoke River Paddle Trail - Conaby Creek

9 Van Swamp Game Land

Morningstar Nature Refuge

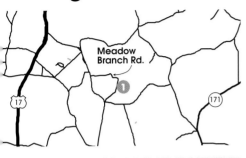

Meadow Branch Rd.

1

17 · 171

Site Information:
Owner: Gail Roberson
1967 Meadow Branch Road,
Williamston, NC 27892
Martin County
252-792-7788
www.morningstarrefuge.org

About the Site:

Although this site is relatively small, about 10 acres in size, there are nice opportunities for birding. Ten short trails, including an observatory overlooking the refuge and swamp, allow easy and quick access to wetland sites typical of eastern North Carolina. The wetland walk bridge across the forested wetland swamp is an especially good spot. Several wetland bird species can be observed or heard here at the appropriate times of year on any given visit, including Prothonotary Warbler, Northern Parula, Yellow-throated Warbler and Summer Tanager. Be on the lookout for Red-shouldered Hawks overhead and listen for the calls of the native Wood Duck. The migration periods can yield especially diverse birding opportunities. Visitors can also enjoy pathways through the private herb, evergreen and perennial gardens on-site to observe other wildlife, study the plant life, or just relax on the studio porch.

Species of Interest: Great Crested Flycatcher, Prothonotary Warbler, Summer Tanager, wading birds, woodpeckers

Habitats: floodplain forest, wetland forest

Special Features/Concerns: Visitors must stay on trails at all times. Pack all trash out and please be quiet. Picking of plants or collection of other natural materials is not permitted. There is a small nature museum on site.

Access & Parking: This site can be accessed daily by appointment only from 2pm until sunset. Visitors must call ahead to schedule a visit. Guided tours can be arranged.

Directions: From US 64 in Williamston, take Exit 514 and travel south on US 17 toward Washington for approximately 2 miles. After the Ready Branch bridge, turn left on Mill Inn Road. After approximately 1.5 miles, where the road splits, bear to the right on Fire Department Road. Travel 0.15 miles, then turn left on Meadow Branch Road. The refuge is 1 mile on the left. Look for a small white sign at the Ready Branch bridge and another pointing the turn to Meadow Branch Road.

Coordinates: N 35°45′46″ W 77°01′25″
DeLorme (NC Gazetteer) Page: 46

Roanoke Group

Morningstar Nature Refuge

Roanoke River Paddle Trail 🛶 🚤 ⛺ 💲 🔫 ❓ 🔭 - Mainstem

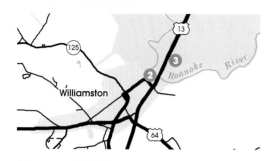

Site Information:
Contact: Roanoke River Partners
Stretch of river between Williamston and
Plymouth, NC; the Roanoke River Partners
office is at 102 North Front Street,
Hamilton, NC 27840
Bertie, Martin, Washington County
252-798-3920
www.roanokeriverpartners.org

About the Site:

This 30 mile section of the Roanoke River
flows through the most extensive bottomland
hardwood forests east of the Mississippi, nearly
all of which are in some sort of conservation
ownership. Designated an Important Bird
Area by Audubon North Carolina, the Roanoke
River is recognized as being globally significant
due to its diversity of birds and amount of vital
habitats for wildlife of all types. The smaller
tributaries and creeks off of the main stem
offer more pristine birding opportunities, especially Gardner Creek/Devil's Gut and Broad
Creek. The main stem can be crowded with
boating activity depending on the season. This
area hosts a variety of breeding wood warblers,
including Cerulean, Swainson's, Prothonotary,
Worm-eating, Kentucky and Hooded Warblers.
Other species found here include Louisiana
Waterthrush, Eastern Wood-Pewee, Wood Duck,
Barred Owl, Anhinga, Bald Eagle, and Mississippi Kite. There are 7 camping platforms
along this section of the river: Conine, Beaver
Lodge (double), Barred Owl Roost, Cypress
Cathedral, Three Sisters, Cow Creek, and Bear

Run. Consult with Roanoke River Partners
to determine appropriate routes and access
points, depending on time constraints and
river conditions.

Species of Interest: Mississippi Kite, Bald
Eagle, Cerulean Warbler, Swainson's Warbler

Habitats: floodplain forest, river

Special Concern: Hunting takes place on
lands along the Roanoke River during certain times of year. Birders should be aware
of current hunting regulations and
seasons and take adequate
safety precautions during
those times. For more on
hunting season safety precautions, see the hunting
season information at the
beginning of this guide.

© Jeff Lewis

Access & Parking: Paddle or
small boat access required. Birders
wishing to paddle portions of the Roanoke
River Paddle Trail should contact Roanoke
River Partners for an official trail guide, map,
and information on current river conditions.
Reservations for overnight camping platforms (fee) must be made in advance. Access points along this stretch of river include:
1) NC Wildlife Resources Commission boat
ramp in Williamston, 2) Roberson Marina
access near Jamesville (Gardner Creek
access), 3) Town of Jamesville access, 4) NC
Wildlife Resources Commission boat ramp in
Plymouth, 5) Town of Plymouth access. Boat
ramp hours vary by ownership.

Directions: To the put-in at Williamston:
From US 64 south of Williamston, take NC
13 north into Williamston. The NC Wildlife
Resources Commission boat ramp is on the
south side of the Roanoke River, just west
of the bridge. Roanoke River Partners can
provide an official trail guide and map.

Coordinates: N 35°51'33" W 77°02'21"
DeLorme (NC Gazetteer) Page: 46

Roanoke Group

Roanoke River National Wildlife ♿ 🚶 🎣 ❓ Refuge - The Kuralt Trail

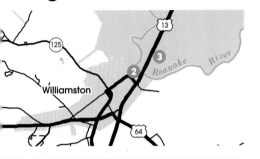

Site Information:
Owner: US Fish and Wildlife Service
US 17/13, approximately 1 mile north of Williamston, NC; Refuge headquarters are at
114 West Water Street, Windsor, NC 27983
Bertie County
252-794-3808
http://roanokeriver.fws.gov

About the Site:

The Roanoke River originates in Virginia and flows through northeastern North Carolina, supporting a floodplain that covers more than 150,000 acres. This region is arguably the most pristine bottomland hardwood system left in the mid-Atlantic region of the United States. Over 219 bird species have been recorded on the floodplain, which supports some of the highest densities of nesting neotropical migratory songbirds in North Carolina. Designated an Important Bird Area by Audubon North Carolina, the Roanoke River is recognized as being globally significant due to its diversity of birds and amount of vital habitats for wildlife of all types. In particular, The Kuralt Trail offers a close look at bottomland hardwood forest and the birds the system supports. Visitors may encounter Cerulean, Swainson's, Prothonotary, Worm-eating, Kentucky and Hooded Warblers, along with other species such as the Mississippi Kite, Barred Owl, American Redstart, or Eastern Wood-Pewee. The trail has numbered stops and a corresponding brochure, as well as interpretive signs. The rest of the Roanoke River National Wildlife Refuge is best accessed by boat from the Roanoke River.

Species of Interest: Mississippi Kite, Cerulean Warbler, American Redstart, Prothonotary Warbler, Swainson's Warbler

Habitats: floodplain forest, pine/hardwood forest

Special Concerns: The entire Roanoke River National Wildlife Refuge spans 5 different tracts along 70 miles of the Roanoke River. Vehicular access is limited. The best access to the refuge is by boat. To inquire about boat access areas, contact the refuge headquarters. The Kuralt Trail and other portions of the refuge are subject to closure for managed hunts during certain times of year. Birders should be aware of current hunting regulations and seasons and take adequate safety precautions during those times. For more on hunting season safety precautions, see the hunting season information at the beginning of this guide. Please contact refuge headquarters for hunt dates and closure information.

Access & Parking: The Kuralt Trail may be accessed during daylight hours, year-round. Interpretive materials are available at the trail head or at the refuge headquarters in Windsor.

Directions: The Kuralt Trail is located approximately 1 mile north of Williamston NC, on north-bound US 17/13. The refuge headquarters are located in downtown Windsor, on the US 17 Bypass (West Water Street).

Coordinates: N 35°52'41" W 77°01'38"
DeLorme (NC Gazetteer) Page: 46

© Walker Golder

Roanoke Group

45

Roanoke River Paddle Trail - Cashie River, Broad Creek

Site Information:
Contact: Roanoke River Partners
Stretch of river between Windsor and the NC 45 bridge; the Roanoke River Partners office is at 102 North Front Street, Hamilton, NC 27840
Bertie County
252-798-3920
www.roanokeriverpartners.org

About the Site:

This 22 mile section of the Cashie River flows through extensive and pristine bottomland hardwood forest, most of which is bordered by NC Wildlife Resources Commission Game Lands. The first 4 miles of the river are narrow and small; the river widens after that. Paddlers may wish to turn around once the river begins to widen in order to make this an out-and-back paddle. The Cashie River, much like the mainstem Roanoke, hosts a variety of breeding wood warblers, including Cerulean, Swainson's, Prothonotary, Worm-eating, Kentucky and Hooded Warblers. Other species found here include Wood Duck, Mississippi Kite, Anhinga, Bald Eagle, and Barred Owl. There are two overnight camping platforms on the Cashie River: Lost Boat and Otter 1. Consult with Roanoke River

© Phil Rhyne

Partners to determine appropriate routes and access points, depending on time constraints and river conditions.

Species of Interest: Mississippi Kite, Bald Eagle, Cerulean Warbler, Swainson's Warbler

Habitats: floodplain forest, river

Special Concern: Hunting takes place on lands along the Cashie River during certain times of year. Birders should be aware of current hunting regulations and seasons and take adequate safety precautions during those times. For more on hunting season safety precautions, see the hunting season information at the beginning of this guide.

Access & Parking: Paddle or small boat access required. Birders wishing to paddle portions of the Roanoke River Paddle Trail and the Cashie River should contact Roanoke River Partners for an official trail guide, map, and information on current river conditions. Reservations for overnight camping platforms (fee) must be made in advance. Access points along this stretch of river include: 1) Roanoke Cashie River Center access in Windsor, 2) NC Wildlife Resources Commission boat ramp in Windsor, 3) NC Wildlife Resources Commission boat ramp in Sans Souci.

Directions: To the put-in in Windsor: take NC 17 business into Windsor, which becomes Water Street. The Roanoke-Cashie River Center is at 112 West Water Street, adjacent to the river. To the take-out at Sans Souci: from Windsor, take NC 17 south for 2.3 miles to Woodward Road. Travel east on Woodward Road for 10.3 miles to the NC Wildlife Resources Commission ramp on the south side of the river, by the Sans Souci ferry. Roanoke River Partners can provide an official trail guide and map.

Coordinates: N 35°59'31" W 76°56'35"
DeLorme (NC Gazetteer) Page: 46

© Harry Sell

Roanoke Group

Cashie Wetlands Walk

♿ 🚶 ⛱ 🚻 ❓ 🔭 🧗

Site Information:
Owner: Town of Windsor
103 North York Street, Windsor, NC 27983
Bertie County
252-794-2331

About the Site:

The Cashie Wetlands Walk features a boardwalk in a natural wetland environment that takes visitors on a comfortable walk through a cypress forest to the edge of the Cashie River, which flows for more than 20 miles through Bertie County. An observation deck along the boardwalk allows for views of wetland birds and other wildlife. Watch and listen for Northern Parula, Prothonotary Warbler, Yellow-throated Warbler, the occasional Barred Owl and a variety of woodpeckers. Along the river, watch for wintering waterfowl during the colder months. This site in the town of Windsor allows for casual birding as well as a chance to enjoy and learn about the history of northeastern North Carolina.

Species of Interest: Prothonotary Warbler, wading birds, wintering waterfowl, woodpeckers

Habitats: floodplain forest, river

Access & Parking: The Cashie Wetlands Walk is accessed beside the Windsor Area Chamber of Commerce building, where parking is available, and is open during daylight hours.

Directions: Take US 17 North from Williamston to Windsor. US 17 becomes Water Street in downtown Windsor. From Water Street, turn left on King Street and go four blocks west to Granville Street. Turn right and travel north on Granville Street for one block. Turn left on York Street and park next to the Windsor Area Chamber of Commerce.

Coordinates: N 35°59'59" W 76°56'43"
DeLorme (NC Gazetteer) Page: 46

6

Historic Hope Plantation

Roanoke Group

excellent information for those interested in the historical heritage of the Roanoke-Chowan regions, especially from 1760-1840. Both resident and migrating songbirds typical of eastern North Carolina mixed hardwood/pine woodlands are possible, such as Great Crested Flycatcher, Red-eyed Vireo, Yellow-throated Warbler, Northern Parula, and Summer Tanager.

Site Information:
Owner: Historic Hope Foundation, Inc.
132 Hope House Road, Windsor, NC 27983
Bertie County
252-794-3140
www.hopeplantation.org

About the Site:

This 46 acre site is managed by the Historic Hope Foundation, Inc. and offers about 18 acres of partially open areas around the buildings and 28 wooded acres with access via 2 short trails. This casual birding stop offers open birding views around the front area and gardens of the site and a chance to stretch your legs on short trails into the woodlands, plus

Species of Interest: Great Crested Flycatcher, Summer Tanager

Habitats: pine/hardwood forest, isolated wetlands, early successional

Special Feature: Registered historic buildings at this site include the grand c. 1803 Hope Mansion, which was the federal-era home of former governor David Stone. This site offers a unique insight into the late 18th and 19th century rural life in eastern North Carolina. A museum room with gift shop and other facilities includes interpretive information on the Hope Mansion and King-Bazemore House.

Access & Parking: The grounds are open daily during daylight hours. The visitor center is open 8:30am to 5pm, Monday - Friday; 10am to 4pm, Saturday; 2pm to 5pm, Sunday. Tours of the historic houses are given 10am to 5pm, Monday - Saturday, and 2pm to 5pm on Sunday (fee). There is no fee for entrance to the visitor center.

Directions: Take US 17 to the US 13 Bypass in Windsor. Turn left on NC 308 for approximately 4 miles, then turn left on Hope House Road. The site is adjacent to South-Western Middle School.

Coordinates: N 36°02'00" W 77°01'03"
DeLorme (NC Gazetteer) Page: 46

Summer Tanager

Rail Switch Nature Trail

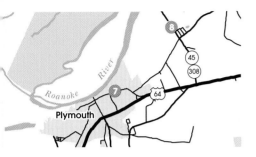

of birds year-round. In the summer, watch for Mississippi Kite, Great Crested Flycatcher, Yellow-throated Vireo, American Redstart, Prothonotary and Swainson's Warbler, among others. Additional possibilities include rails, wading birds and wintering waterfowl. The nature trail features educational signs and displays about the Roanoke River and its wildlife. Park benches, picnic tables and a boat dock offer additional recreational options and the trail system is right next to downtown Plymouth.

Site Information:
Owner: Town of Plymouth
East Water Street, Plymouth, NC 27962
Washington County
252-793-9101
www.visitplymouthnc.com

About the Site:

The Rail Switch Nature Trail is a little over 0.3 miles long and includes an extensive walkable section adjacent to the Roanoke River, with boardwalks and 3 observation decks. These areas provide excellent views of wooded and marshland habitats, as well as the river itself. Across the river from the trail is the Bachelor Bay Game Land, with extensive marsh, swamp forest and cypress-tupelo and bottomland hardwood forest habitats that support a variety

Species of Interest: Mississippi Kite, Great Crested Flycatcher, American Redstart, Prothonotary Warbler, Swainson's Warbler, wintering waterfowl

Habitats: pine/hardwood forest, floodplain forest, river

Access & Parking: The trail can be accessed during daylight hours, year-round. Parking is available at the trail head.

Directions: From US 64 in Plymouth, turn left on Washington Street and follow it toward the river until it dead-ends into Water Street. Turn right and travel east on Water Street. The trail is located at the east end of Water Street.

Coordinates: N 35°52′09″ W 76°44′39″
DeLorme (NC Gazetteer) Page: 46

Roanoke Group

Rail Switch Nature Trail

Roanoke River Paddle Trail - Conaby Creek

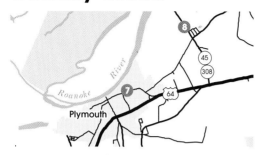

among others. Waterfowl, including Blue-winged Teal, use the area in the winter. Consult with Roanoke River Partners to determine appropriate routes and access points, depending on time constraints and river conditions.

Site Information:
Contact: Roanoke River Partners
Put-in at NC 45/308, Conaby Creek Bridge; the Roanoke River Partners office is at 102 North Front Street, Hamilton, NC 27840
Washington County
252-798-3920
www.roanokeriverpartners.org

About the Site:

Conaby Creek empties into the Roanoke River just before the main river enters the Albemarle Sound. This 3 mile stretch of river, from the put-in on NC 45/308, to the Royal Fern camping platform on White Marsh Creek, passes through tidal swamp forest and dense shrubland habitat. Watch and listen for Wood Duck, Bald Eagle, Osprey, Northern Parula, Yellow-throated Warbler, and Summer Tanager,

Osprey in flight

Species of Interest: Bald Eagle, Summer Tanager, wintering waterfowl

Habitats: floodplain forest, moist shrubland, river

Special Concern: Hunting takes place on lands along the Roanoke River and its tributaries during certain times of year. Birders should be aware of current hunting regulations and seasons and take adequate safety precautions during those times. For more on hunting season safety precautions, see the hunting season information at the beginning of this guide. This section of the river is in the heart of bear country. Campers MUST follow all protocols for camping in bear country with special attention given to food and trash storage.

Access & Parking: Paddle or small boat access required. Birders wishing to paddle Conaby Creek should contact Roanoke River Partners for an official trail guide, map, and information on current river conditions. Reservations for overnight camping platforms (fee) must be made in advance. The access point along this stretch of river is at the NC Wildlife Resources Commission boat ramp on NC 45/308.

Directions: From the intersection of NC 32 and US 64 in Plymouth, travel east on US 64 for 3 miles to NC 45/308. Travel north on NC 45/308 for 1.8 miles to the NC Wildlife Resources Commission boat ramp at Conaby Creek. Roanoke River Partners can provide an official trail guide and map.

Coordinates: N 35°53'44" W 76°42'18"
DeLorme (NC Gazetteer) Page: 46

Roanoke Group

Van Swamp Game Land

Site Information:
Owner: NC Wildlife Resources Commission
NC 32, south of Plymouth, NC
Washington/Beaufort County line
252-792-3868
www.ncwildlife.org

About the Site:
Van Swamp Game Land consists largely of hardwood swamp forest and dense shrubland habitats that are virtually impenetrable on foot. The birding opportunities here are therefore limited to the roads that traverse the property. Listen for Black-throated Green Warbler, Swainson's Warbler and other migrating and breeding birds associated with swamp forest. Begin along Church Road, at the southern end of the property. Turn north on Pocosin Boulevard for 2 miles, then west on Hollis Loop Road. This road (which becomes Turkey Lane Road) ends at Railroad Road, which then heads northwest for 0.5 miles until its terminus

at Hollis Road. Turn right on Hollis Road and follow it back out to NC 32. Thinned pine stands along Hollis Road, on the north side of the property, offer opportunities to bird in more open habitat. Listen for Northern Bobwhite, Brown-headed Nuthatch, Pine Warbler and other birds of pine woodlands.

Species of Interest: Brown-headed Nuthatch, Black-throated Green Warbler, Swainson's Warbler

Habitats: pine/hardwood forest, moist shrubland, early successional

Special Concern: Hunting is allowed on Game Lands during certain times of year. Birders should be aware of current hunting regulations and seasons and take adequate safety precautions during those times. For more on hunting season safety precautions, see the hunting season information at the beginning of this guide.

Access & Parking: It is highly recommended that visitors request a current Game Lands Map Book from the NC Wildlife Resources Commission before visiting. Vehicle access to roads may vary seasonally; the roads are closed March 1 - September 1. There are no designated parking areas on Van Swamp Game Land. Visitors can park on roadsides but should be aware of conditions and stay on roads that are in passable condition. Road conditions can vary greatly depending on the amount of recent rainfall and use on the Game Lands.

Directions: From Washington, take US 264 east for just over 6 miles. Turn north on NC 32 and travel for just under 17 miles. Turn left on Church Road just before Long Acre Church to access the Game Land.

Coordinates: N 35°41'40" W 76°46'21"
DeLorme (NC Gazetteer) Page: 46

Brown-headed Nuthatch

 Roanoke Group

© Brady Beck

Red-headed Woodpecker

While You're In the Area

Historic Albemarle Tour, Inc.
NC Heritage Trail
PO Box 1604
Washington, NC 27889
800-734-1117
www.historicnenc.com

HomegrownHandmade
Art Roads and Farm Trails of North Carolina
www.homegrownhandmade.com

Roanoke/Cashie River Center
112 W. Water Street
Windsor, NC 27983
252-796-1000
www.partnershipforthesounds.org/rcrc_home.htm

Roanoke River Lighthouse and Maritime Museum
East Water Street
Plymouth, NC 27962
252-793-1377

Roanoke River Paddle Trail
Roanoke River Partners
102 North Front Street
Hamilton, NC 27840
252-792-3790
www.roanokeriverpartners.org

Sylvan Heights Waterfowl Park & Eco-Center
4963 Hwy 258
Scotland Neck, NC 27874
252-826-3186
http://shwpark.com

Welcome to the
Albemarle Peninsula Group

The Albemarle Peninsula abounds with wildlife refuges, parks, game lands and conservation areas. These protected habitats range from wetlands and cypress swamps to bottomland forests and managed agricultural fields, making the peninsula a magnet for both summer and winter birds. Tens of thousands of waterfowl make the peninsula their winter home. Summer brings an abundance of nesting songbirds, making this area a premier east coast birding location year-round.

You Are Here

Raleigh

© John Ennis

Albemarle Peninsula Group

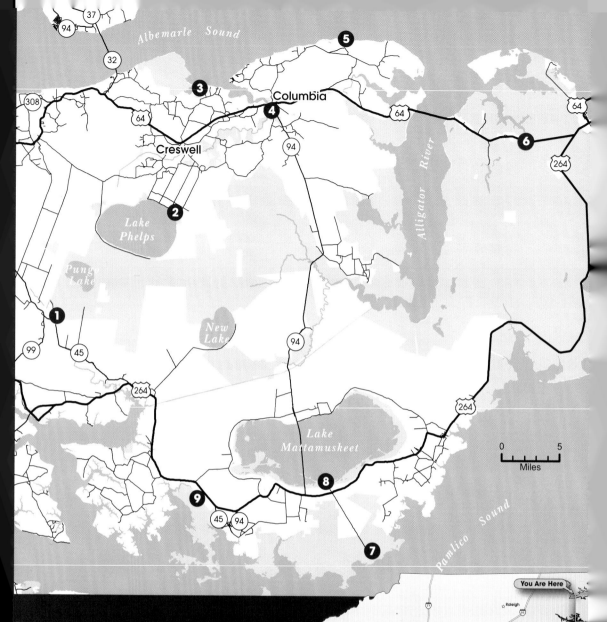

Albemarle Peninsula Group

1 Pocosin Lakes National Wildlife Refuge

2 Pettigrew State Park

3 Eastern 4-H Environmental Education
   Conference Center

4 Scuppernong River Interpretive Trail

5 Palmetto Peartree Preserve

6 Alligator River National Wildlife Refuge

7 Gull Rock Game Land

8 Mattamuskeet National Wildlife Refuge

9 Swanquarter National Wildlife Refuge

ocosin Lakes National Wildlife Refuge

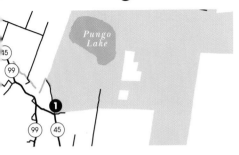

and red wolves have been reintroduced. It is strongly recommended that you have a refuge map when visiting.

© John Hammond

Snow Geese at Pocosin Lakes
National Wildlife Refuge

Site Information:
Owner: US Fish and Wildlife Service
NC 45, south of Plymouth, NC. Refuge headquarters are located at 205 South Ludington Drive, Columbia, NC 27925
Tyrrell, Washington, and Hyde Counties
252-796-3004
www.fws.gov/pocosinlakes/

bout the Site:
med for the Algonquian word meaning vamp on a hill," Pocosin Lakes National ldlife Refuge is home to thousands of winter-g waterfowl that graze farm fields by day and ost on lakes by night. The Pungo Unit of e refuge is the most accessible and reliable r waterfowl. During late fall and winter onths, more than 80,000 Tundra Swan and ow Goose can be seen leaving Pungo Lake huge flocks at dawn and returning at dusk. ads leading to the lake pass open fields and npoundments that provide opportunities to ew foraging waterfowl and raptors. Canals ed with shrubby vegetation along the roads e home to Wood Duck, sparrows, and other eeding songbirds. The observation tower on e south edge of the lake is a good place to ew the lake; waterfowl are typically seen at a stance. The Pungo Unit is most productive winter but more than 200 species have been ted on the refuge. In other seasons, watch r Northern Bobwhite, Eastern Kingbird, digo Bunting and in the woods by the lake, othonotary Warbler. The remainder of this st refuge can be explored from the many ads. Black bear can be seen on the refuge

Species of Interest: Snow Goose, Tundra Swan, wintering waterfowl

Habitats: moist shrubland, wetland forest, lake

Special Concern: If visiting after heavy rains, some roads will require 4-wheel drive. Hunting is allowed on the refuge during certain times of year. Birders should be aware of current hunting regulations and seasons and take adequate safety precautions during those times. For more on hunting season safety precautions, see the hunting season information at the beginning of this guide.

Access & Parking: The refuge has more than 100 miles of roads that run through a variety of habitats. The best access point for birding is at the Pungo Unit on the south shore of Pungo Lake. It is strongly suggested that visitors pick up a brochure and map at the refuge headquarters in Columbia or at the field station on Shore Drive. The refuge is open during daylight hours, year round. Unimproved roads may be accessed on foot.

Directions: To reach the Pungo Unit, take NC 45 south from Plymouth. NC 45 merges with NC 99 for approximately 11 miles before they split again. When the NC 99/45 split occurs, bear left on NC 45 and shortly thereafter, look for the refuge entrance on the north side of the road.

Coordinates: N 35°39'30" W 76°35'31"
DeLorme (NC Gazetteer) Page: 47

55

Great Crested Flycatcher

Pettigrew State Park

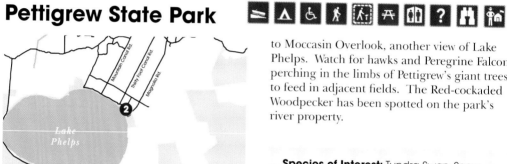

Albemarle Peninsula Group

Site Information:
Owner: NC State Parks
2252 Lake Shore Road, Creswell, NC 27928
Washington and Tyrrell Counties
252-797-4475
www.ncsparks.net

About the Site:
Pettigrew State Park includes 1,278 acres of land around Lake Phelps, 16,600 acres of water (Lake Phelps) and over 2,600 acres on the Scuppernong River. From the park office, take the Bee Tree Trail through a sweetgum forest; watch and listen for breeding songbirds, including Yellow-billed Cuckoo, Acadian Flycatcher, Northern Parula, Ovenbird, and Indigo Bunting. This trail leads to a wooden overlook offering a view of Lake Phelps and a place to observe wintering waterfowl. A variety of woodpeckers can also be spotted here. Moccasin Trail leads northwest from the park office for 3 miles to Moccasin Canal. This trail passes through cypress and hardwood forests before reaching a 350 foot boardwalk, which leads

to Moccasin Overlook, another view of Lake Phelps. Watch for hawks and Peregrine Falcon perching in the limbs of Pettigrew's giant trees to feed in adjacent fields. The Red-cockaded Woodpecker has been spotted on the park's river property.

Species of Interest: Tundra Swan, Snow Goose, Bald Eagle, Peregrine Falcon, wintering waterfowl

Habitats: floodplain forest, moist shrubland, lake

Special Feature: Pettigrew is also home to award-winning big trees - several species in the park are national or state tree champions! Learn more about these trees at the park's annual Big Tree Walk in November.

Access & Parking: Parking is available at the park office on Lake Shore Road, Pocosin Overlook, and at the Cypress Point access area. The park is open from 8am to 6pm, November - February; 8am to 7pm, March and October; 8am to 8pm, April, May, and September; 8am to 9pm, June - August.

Directions: Pettigrew State Park is located seven miles south of Creswell off US 64. From US 64, take the Alligood Road exit and travel south. Follow the directional signs to the park office.

Coordinates: N 35°47'26" W 76°24'23"
DeLorme (NC Gazetteer) Page: 47

Eastern 4-H Environmental Education Conference Center

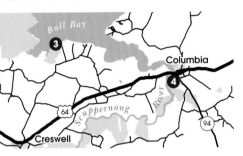

Site Information:
Owner: NC State University
100 North Clover Way, Columbia, NC 27925
Tyrrell County
252-797-4800
www.eastern4hcenter.org

About the Site:

Take any of the Center's numerous paths and trails to look and listen for birds. These paths cross through both upland pine and hardwood areas, as well as open fields and along tree lines - these areas provide a good opportunity to watch for wintering sparrows. An early morning visit during the spring or fall migration may provide the best birding opportunities. Also watch and listen for Ovenbird, Yellow-throated Warbler, and Blue-gray Gnatcatcher during the breeding season. A boardwalk extends along the shoreline west of the Conference Center; this area may present good opportunities to see or hear wetland associated species such as Prothonotary Warbler and Northern Parula, along with other migrating or breeding songbirds. In the winter, head toward the pier on the Albemarle Sound to scan for wintering waterfowl and be on the lookout for a Bald Eagle overhead.

Species of Interest: Bald Eagle, Great Crested Flycatcher, Prothonotary Warbler, wintering waterfowl

Habitats: pine/hardwood forest, early successional, sound

Access & Parking: This site is open year round, but it is accessible only by appointment. Call ahead to schedule your visit. Primary access is during spring and fall; most trails are inaccessible during summer camp season. Birding club and group accommodation reservations are seasonally available. Park in the Conference Center lot. The boardwalk, paved, and wooded trails can all be accessed on foot from the main building complex. Daily hours of operation are 8am to 5pm. Some amenities are only available Monday - Friday.

Directions: From US 64 just west of Columbia, take exit 562 - Travis Road/Bay Post Office Road. Travel north approximately 3 miles, where the road ends at Albemarle Church Road. Turn right on Albemarle Church Road and travel for 1 mile. Turn left on Bulls Bay Road and the Center's entrance is on the left.

Coordinates: N 35°56'08" W 76°21'24"
DeLorme (NC Gazetteer) Page: 47

Eastern 4-H Environmental Education Center boardwalk

Albemarle Peninsula Group

57

Scuppernong River Interpretive Trail

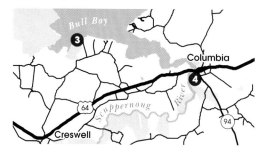

Site Information:
Owner: US Fish and Wildlife Service
and The Partnership for the Sounds
205 South Ludington Drive, Columbia,
NC 27925
Tyrrell County
252-796-3004

About the Site:

The Scuppernong River Interpretive Trail boardwalk begins directly behind the Walter B. Jones Sr. Center for the Sounds and the Tyrrell County Visitor Center. It follows along the edge of the Scuppernong River for a short distance before entering a cypress swamp. Watch for wintering waterfowl and various wading birds along the river's edge. As you enter the cypress swamp, listen for Northern Parula, Prothonotary Warbler, Hooded Warbler and other breeding and migrating songbirds. Fourteen interpretive signs along the trail explain the unique features and characteristics of the area. The boardwalk splits shortly after entering the cypress swamp; either pathway will bring you to an observation deck a short distance down the Scuppernong River shoreline. The entire boardwalk is 0.75 miles in length.

Species of Interest: Prothonotary Warbler, Hooded Warbler, wading birds, wintering waterfowl

Habitats: floodplain forest, river

Special Feature: The boardwalk is designated as a National Recreational Trail by the Secretary of the Interior and contains the NC Champion Big Tree for the Carolina Ash.

Access & Parking: Park in the lot shared by the Pocosin Lakes National Wildlife Refuge headquarters, the Walter B. Jones Sr. Center for the Sounds and the Tyrrell County Visitor Center. The boardwalk begins directly behind the refuge headquarters building, along the river. The boardwalk can be accessed year round during daylight hours. The Walter B. Jones Sr. Center for the Sounds is open at varying times during the week, depending on volunteer staff availability.

Directions: From points west, enter Columbia by crossing the Scuppernong River on US 64. Make the first right turn at the Tyrrell County Visitors Center, which is easily visible from the road. The Pocosin Lakes National Wildlife Refuge headquarters and the Walter B. Jones Sr. Center for the Sounds, where the boardwalk begins, are adjacent to the visitor center.

Coordinates: N 35°54'55" W 76°15'12"
DeLorme (NC Gazetteer) Page: 47

Hooded Warbler

5

Palmetto-Peartree Preserve

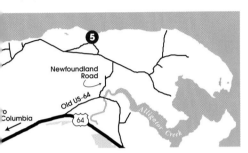

Site Information:
Owner: The Conservation Fund
Pot Licker Road, northeast of Columbia, NC
Tyrrell County
919-967-2223 or locally, 252-796-0723
www.palmettopeartree.org

About the Site:

This 10,000-acre preserve, locally known as P3, is in a remote location along the banks of the Albemarle Sound and Alligator River. Designated as an Important Bird Area by Audubon NC, it is home to the Red-cockaded Woodpecker, with more than 100 nesting cavities and 28 clusters of birds. A map on P3's website shows the locations of some accessible cavity trees, which are marked with a painted white circle. P3's habitat is a diverse mix of bottomland swamps, hardwood-pine forest and marsh. Birders can look and listen for more than 100 species of migratory and breeding birds that use the preserve each year, including Prothonotary, Worm-eating, and Swainson's Warblers. Several boardwalk trails and an extensive network of dirt logging roads provide easy access throughout the preserve. Two sections of the Shoreline Trail have interpretive signage and take you through a wetland forest to Albemarle Sound. The 0.75 mile Woodland Trail has two wildlife viewing stations and winds through pine forest. A paddling trail

© Jeff Lewis

and camping platform on Hidden Lake adds another dimension to this site. P3 is also home to American alligators, red wolves, bobcats, black bears, and white-tailed deer.

Species of Interest: Bald Eagle, Red-cockaded Woodpecker, Prothonotary Warbler, Worm-eating Warbler, Swainson's Warbler

Habitats: pine/hardwood forest, floodplain forest, isolated wetlands, sound

Special Concern: The federally endangered Red-cockaded Woodpecker can be found on site year round. Observe all interpretive signage and do not disturb the birds. Hunting is allowed on the preserve during certain times of the year; hunting areas will be posted on the preserve's website. Birders should be aware of current hunting regulations and seasons and take adequate safety precautions during those times. For more on hunting season safety precautions, see the hunting season information at the beginning of this guide.

Access & Parking: From the preserve entrance, follow the signs to the boardwalk and canoe launches. The preserve is open from dawn to dusk, year round. Reservations to use the canoe camping platform on Hidden Lake can be made through Roanoke River Partners (www.roanokeriverpartners.org). The boat ramp can only accommodate canoes and kayaks.

Directions: From Columbia, travel 5 miles east on US 64. Turn north onto Old US 64 (SR 1229). After approximately 2 miles, turn north on Newfoundland Road (SR 1221) and continue for several miles to the dead end at Soundside Road (SR 1209). Turn west on Soundside Road, travel approximately 0.8 miles, and turn right onto Pot Licker Road (SR 1220). The marked entrance to the preserve is on the right.

Coordinates: N 35°59'17" W 76°08'03"
DeLorme (NC Gazetteer) Page: 48

Albemarle Peninsula Group

6

Alligator River National Wildlife Refuge

Albemarle Peninsula Group

Site Information:
Owner: US Fish and Wildlife Service
US 64, west of Manns Harbor, NC
Dare County
252-473-1131
www.fws.gov/alligatorriver

About the Site:

Over 150,000 acres in size, and with 250 bird species documented, this refuge offers many opportunities for birders in a diversity of coastal plain habitats. From April to June, most of the refuge's breeding birds can be found along the two-mile Buffalo City Road that ends at the Sandy Ridge Wildlife Trail. There you will find an observation tower overlooking Milltail Creek. This location is also the put-in for the refuge's four paddle trails. Listen for Swainson's Warbler and other breeding songbirds in this area. At the refuge entrance on Milltail Road, Creef Cut Trail provides access for viewing wintering waterfowl on the flooded impoundments. A Short-eared Owl is a possibility at dusk. Milltail Road traverses extensive farm fields and impoundments where raptors

Short-eared Owl

and waterfowl can be seen, but often at some distance from the road. Along the roadside, check for winter sparrows. Beyond the farm fields, birding is best during the breeding season. In early morning, black bear can likely be found in this area. Continue on Milltail Road to exit the refuge on US 264 and travel west to access the southern portion of the refuge. This area offers excellent birding during the spring and summer.

Species of Interest: Short-eared Owl, Brown-headed Nuthatch, Swainson's Warbler, winter sparrows, winter waterfowl

Habitats: pine/hardwood forest, early successional, moist shrubland, managed waterfowl impoundments

Special Concern: Hunting is allowed on the refuge during certain times of year. Birders should be aware of current hunting regulations and seasons and take adequate safety precautions during those times. For more on hunting season safety precautions, see the hunting season information at the beginning of this guide.

Access & Parking: The refuge contains more than 100 miles of roads that run through a variety of habitats. The main access points are Milltail Road and Buffalo City Road. Parking areas are designated at three sites in the refuge: the Milltail Road entrance, farther south on Milltail Road where it crosses Milltail Creek, and at the Sandy Ridge Wildlife Trail, off of Buffalo City Road. It is strongly suggested that visitors pick up a refuge brochure at the Milltail Road kiosk for a detailed site map and trail information. The refuge is open during daylight hours, year round.

Directions: Alligator River National Wildlife Refuge covers an extensive area with multiple access routes. To find the main trail and visitor opportunities, travel west from Manns Harbor on US 64/264. Approximately 4 miles west of the US 64/264 split, turn south onto Milltail Road. This entrance serves as

(continues)

the trail head for Creef Cut Wildlife Trail and is the north entrance of the road designated as the Wildlife Drive. Here you will find refuge brochures and an informational kiosk. Continuing west on US 64, approximately 3.2 miles past Milltail Road, turn south on Buffalo City Road to access the Sandy Ridge Wildlife Trail and paddle trails at the end of the road.

Coordinates: N 35°51'50" W 75°51'38"
DeLorme (NC Gazetteer) Page: 48

7

Gull Rock Game Land

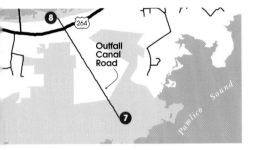

Blue Grosbeak

© John Ennis

Species of Interest: Chuck-will's-widow, Marsh Wren, Blue Grosbeak, wintering waterfowl

Habitats: early successional, moist shrubland, salt marsh, managed waterfowl impoundments

Special Concern: Hunting is allowed on Game Lands during certain times of year. Birders should be aware of current hunting regulations and seasons and take adequate safety precautions during those times. For more on hunting season safety precautions, see the hunting season information at the beginning of this guide.

Access & Parking: Parking is designated at both ends of the waterfowl impoundment on Loop Road. However, the Game Land entrance gate to reach Loop Road is closed March 1 - September 1. During this time period, park along Outfall Canal Road, near the Loop Road turn. It is highly recommended that visitors request a current Game Lands Map Book from the NC Wildlife Resources Commission before visiting. Visitors can park on roadsides but should be aware of conditions and stay on roads that are in passable condition. Road conditions can vary greatly depending on the amount of recent rainfall and use on the Game Lands.

Directions: Take US 264 east of Swan Quarter to New Holland, just south of Lake Mattamuskeet. Turn right on Outfall Canal Road (SR 1164). The Game Land boundary begins at 4.3 miles. Loop Road, which leads to a managed waterfowl impoundment, turns off to the left at approximately 5 miles.

Coordinates: N 35°22'41" W 76°06'44"
DeLorme (NC Gazetteer) Page: 68

Site Information:
Owner: NC Wildlife Resources Commission
Outfall Canal Road (SR 1164), east of Swan Quarter, NC
Hyde County
252-482-7701
www.ncwildlife.org

About the Site:

Gull Rock Game Land can be a nice additional stop on a visit to Mattamuskeet National Wildlife Refuge, especially in winter and during the breeding season (April-June). The birding opportunities here are mostly by car, along the primary road in the Game Land, Outfall Canal Road. Drive along Outfall Canal Road and watch for early successional species in the nearby fields, including Indigo Bunting, Blue Grosbeak, and various sparrows. Listen for Chuck-will's-widows and various warblers in the wooded sections. Loop Road and West Green Road offer additional driving opportunities, if access is permitted. Otherwise, walk these roads on foot. Loop Road leads 0.5 miles to a managed waterfowl impoundment. Near the boat ramp at the end of Outfall Canal Road, scan for marsh birds, including Marsh Wren and rails.

Albemarle Peninsula Group

8

Mattamuskeet National Wildlife Refuge

Tundra Swan

© Jeff Lewis

Mattamuskeet is not complete without a sunset view from NC 94 as thousands of Tundra Swan return to the lake from a day of foraging in local farm fields.

Site Information:
Owner: US Fish and Wildlife Service
NC 94, just south of Fairfield, NC
Hyde County
252-926-4021
www.fws.gov/mattamuskeet/

About the Site:

Lake Mattamuskeet, the largest natural freshwater lake in North Carolina, is the refuge's main feature. Its shallow depth creates a magnet for wintering waterfowl. Nearby marsh, swamp forest and cropland attract a diversity of songbirds. Although birding can be good at Mattamuskeet year round, it is most productive from mid-November through January, when wintering waterfowl are present in large numbers. The entrance road, Wildlife Drive, and the NC 94 causeway, as it crosses the lake, offer some of the best and most accessible birding opportunities. Wooded areas along these drives are productive for migrating and breeding birds. The NC 94 observation platform just north of the entrance drive offers unobstructed views of the lake. The New Holland Trail boardwalk from East Canal Drive provides access to a cypress swamp and marsh. Additional points on the east side of the lake offer access but some require extensive walks to reach the lake. Lake Landing is one of the most accessible. The west side of the lake provides seasonal boat access and access to additional impoundments and forest habitats. Paddling this area in early spring can provide good birding and views of lingering waterfowl. A winter trip to

Species of Interest: Tundra Swan, Snow Goose, Bald Eagle, migrating shorebirds, wintering waterfowl

Habitats: pine/hardwood forest, wetland forest, isolated wetlands, lake

Special Concern: Hunting is allowed on the refuge during certain times of the year. Birders should be aware of current hunting regulations and seasons and take adequate safety precautions during those times. For more on hunting season safety precautions, see the hunting season information at the beginning of this guide. A total of 30 miles of levees and 15 miles of roads are available to the public on the refuge. However, some levees and roads are closed to public use from November 1 - February 28, restricting winter visits to 8 miles of levee and 12 miles of roads.

Access & Parking: There are multiple access areas on the refuge. The main access points are the entrance road, East Canal Drive (behind refuge headquarters), and NC 94 as it crosses Lake Mattamuskeet. Observation areas are designated along the entrance road and on NC 94. It is strongly suggested that visitors pick up a brochure at refuge headquarters for a detailed site map. The refuge is open during daylight hours, year round.

Directions: From US 264 between Swan Quarter and Englehard, turn north onto NC 94. The refuge entrance is 1.5 miles north of the intersection, on the right.

Coordinates: N 35°27'07" W 76°10'38"
DeLorme (NC Gazetteer) Page: 68

Swanquarter National Wildlife Refuge

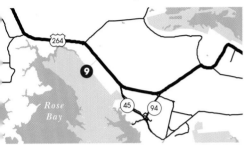

Site Information:
Owner: US Fish and Wildlife Service
On Pamlico Sound, west of Swan Quarter, NC
Hyde County
252-926-4021
www.fws.gov/swanquarter/

About the Site:

Mainland access to the refuge, the Bell Island Unit, is gained via a gravel road that extends from US 264 south to the Pamlico Sound. This road provides visual access to the marsh, estuarine loblolly pine forest, and Pamlico Sound. Swanquarter National Wildlife Refuge is most noted for wintering waterfowl, particularly diving ducks. The two mile drive from US 264 to the fishing pier is worth a few stops for migrating songbirds; Brown-headed Nuthatch is a year round possibility. The 1,000 foot fishing pier provides views to the upper portion

of Rose Bay for waterfowl. Waterfowl are most abundant in late winter and lighting is best in early morning. At the fishing pier, Bufflehead, Canvasback, and Hooded and Red-breasted Merganser are possibilities. The marsh around the parking lot should be checked for Sedge Wren and winter sparrows.

Species of Interest: Canvasback, Hooded Merganser, Brown-headed Nuthatch, Sedge Wren

Habitats: pine/hardwood forest, wetland forest, salt marsh, sound

Special Concern: Hunting is allowed on the refuge during certain times of year. Birders should be aware of current hunting regulations and seasons and take adequate safety precautions during those times. For more on hunting season safety precautions, see the hunting season information at the beginning of this guide.

Access & Parking: Swanquarter National Wildlife Refuge is open during daylight hours, year round. Parking is available at the fishing pier at the end of the entrance road. Most of the refuge is accessible only by boat, except for the Bell Island Unit. Pedestrian access is permitted if the gate is closed but parking is very limited and the gate should not be blocked. It is strongly suggested that visitors pick up a brochure and site map at the Mattamuskeet National Wildlife Refuge headquarters, located east of Swan Quarter.

Directions: From the intersection of NC 45 and US 264 west of Swan Quarter, continue west on US 264/45 for approximately 1.5 miles. Turn south on the gravel road marked by the refuge sign. The road ends on Pamlico Sound in the Bell Island Unit.

Coordinates: N 35°26'35" W 76°22'35"
DeLorme (NC Gazetteer) Page: 67

© Phil Rhyne

Hooded Merganser

© Mark Buckler

Sunrise at Pocosin Lakes National Wildlife Refuge

© John Ennis

Historic Mattamuskeet Lodge and pump station

While You're In the Area

Bayview – Aurora Ferry
NC Department of Transportation, Ferry Division
252-964-4521
www.ncdot.org/transit/ferry

Fort Raleigh National Historic Site
National Park Service
1401 National Park Drive
Manteo, North Carolina 27954
252-473-5772
www.nps.gov/fora

Historic Albemarle Tour, Inc.
NC Heritage Trail
PO Box 1604
Washington, NC 27889
800-734-1117
www.historicnenc.com

HomegrownHandmade
Art Roads and Farm Trails of North Carolina
www.homegrownhandmade.com

North Carolina Aquarium at Roanoke Island
374 Airport Road
Manteo, North Carolina 27954-0967
866-332-3475
www.ncaquariums.com/ri/riindex.htm

North Carolina Maritime Museum on Roanoke Island
106 Fernando Street
Manteo, NC 27954
252-475-1750
www.ah.dcr.state.nc.us/sections/maritime/
branches/roanoke_default.htm

Pocosin Arts Center
Main Street
Columbia, NC 27925
252-796-2787
www.pocosinarts.org

Swan Quarter – Ocracoke Ferry
NC Department of Transportation, Ferry Division
800-773-1094
www.ncdot.org/transit/ferry

Welcome to the
Outer Banks Group

Some of the finest birding opportunities that exist on the Atlantic Coast are found in the Outer Banks. This area includes ea Island National Wildlife Refuge, an almost ,000-acre barrier island. Wading birds, waerfowl, shorebirds, terns, gulls and salt marsh ongbirds are abundant year-round at the efuge and along the upper sections of Cape Hatteras National Seashore. Both of these areas are globally recognized as Important Bird Areas by Audubon. Sites in this group feature outstanding birding opportunities at fresh and saltwater marshes, barrier island dunes, and ocean and sound side shorelines. Rarities are commonplace, and spring and fall migrations can offer spectacular birding experiences.

You Are Here

77

☆ Raleigh

95

© Brady Beck

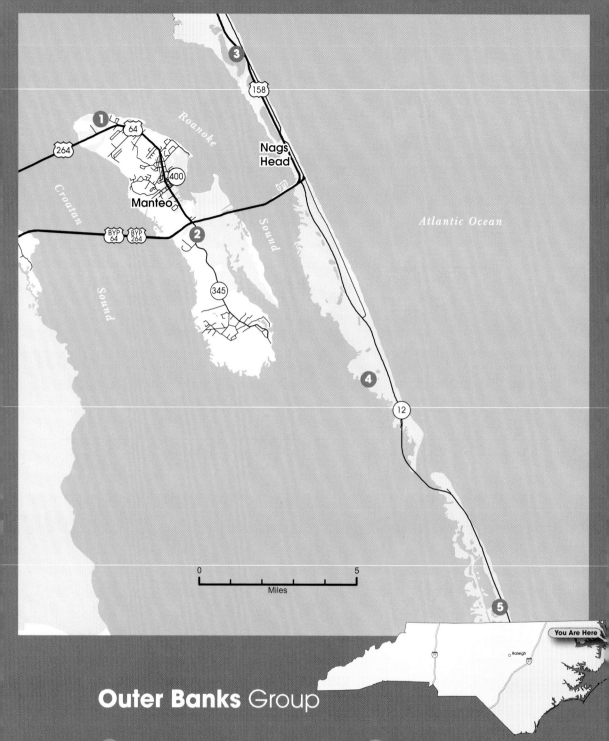

Roanoke

158

Nags Head

64
264
64
400
Manteo
BYP 64
BYP 264

Croatan
Sound

345

Sound

Atlantic Ocean

12

4

5

0   5
Miles

You Are Here

77
Raleigh
95

Outer Banks Group

1 The Elizabethan Gardens

2 Roanoke Island Marsh Game Land

3 Jockey's Ridge State Park

4 Cape Hatteras National Seashore - Bodie Island

5 Pea Island National Wildlife Refuge

The Elizabethan Gardens

$ ♿   ⛺   🚻   ❓   🧍

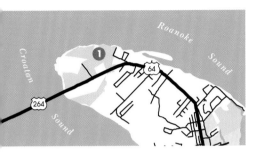

Site Information:
Owner: The Elizabethan Gardens
1411 National Park Drive, Manteo, NC 27954
Dare County
252-473-3234
www.elizabethangardens.org

About the Site:

The Elizabethan Gardens is a private, non-profit public garden managed by The Garden Club of North Carolina. The gardens consist of 10.5 acres of oak forest interspersed with loblolly pine, southern magnolia, and American holly. There are well-marked trails meandering through the gardens, most of which are wheelchair accessible. Over 175 species of birds have been seen in or from the Elizabethan Gardens. Spring and fall are the best seasons to visit. In the springtime, arrive early and stroll the well-manicured paths. Listen for Northern Parula, Black-throated Green, Black-and-white, and Prairie Warblers, along with many other warblers, vireos and other migrants. During the fall, clear skies and northwest winds bring lots of migrant songbirds to the Gardens. Tanagers, grosbeaks, orioles, thrushes, vireos and a variety of warblers pass through, especially in September and October. In winter look for loons, grebes, diving ducks, pelicans and terns from the Gazebo or from the Watergate path. Roanoke Sound hosts hundreds of Bufflehead in winter and Common Goldeneye is a possibility. The moderate winter temperatures on Roanoke Island allow a small number of Ruby-throated Hummingbirds and sometimes a migrant warbler or two to over-winter here. The Gardens also host a variety of regular summer

breeders, including Yellow-billed Cuckoo, Great Crested Flycatcher, Brown-headed Nuthatch, Pileated Woodpecker, and White-eyed Vireo.

© Jeff Lewis

Brown-headed Nuthatch

Species of Interest: Great Crested Flycatcher, Magnolia Warbler, Black-throated Blue Warbler, Brown-headed Nuthatch, Baltimore Oriole, wintering waterfowl

Habitats: pine/hardwood forest, maritime forest, beach

Special Feature: The Elizabethan Gardens appeal to horticulturists, nature-lovers, and history buffs alike. This historical setting is the site of the first English colony in the New World. The Gardens include period English furniture and portraits, Italian Renaissance statuary and the world's largest bronze sculpture of HRH Queen Elizabeth I.

Access & Parking: The Elizabethan Gardens are located adjacent to the Fort Raleigh National Historic Site and the Lost Colony Theatre grounds. The gardens are open daily from 9am to 5pm, year-round, except for major holidays (seasonal extended hours). An entrance fee is required. Concessions are available at the gift shop.

Directions: From downtown Manteo, travel west on old US 264 for approximately 4 miles. Turn right at the entrance to the Fort Raleigh National Historic Site and the Lost Colony Theatre. The Elizabethan Gardens are located in the same complex. From the west on US 64, turn left in Mann's Harbor at the foot of the Virginia Dare Bridge. Proceed through Mann's Harbor and cross the William B. Umstead Bridge. Approximately one mile beyond the bridge watch for signs for Fort Raleigh National Historic Site, The Lost Colony Theatre and The Elizabethan Gardens.

Coordinates: N 35°56′13″ W 75°42′41″
DeLorme (NC Gazetteer) Page: 49

Outer Banks Group

Roanoke Island Marsh Game Land ♿ 🚶 🔫 🔭

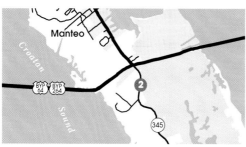

Manteo

Site Information:
Owner: NC Wildlife Resources Commission
NC 345, south of Manteo, NC
Dare County
252-482-7701
www.ncwildlife.org

King Rail

About the Site:
From the parking area, follow the 0.3 mile long loop walking trail, which leads to views of a 40-acre waterfowl impoundment and a black needle-rush marsh. During winter, birders will have opportunities to see waterfowl such as Tundra Swan, Mallard, American Black Duck, Gadwall, Northern Pintail, American Wigeon, Green-winged Teal and Hooded Merganser. During warmer months, look for Glossy and White Ibis, Osprey and wading birds in the marsh, waterfowl impoundment, and tidal creeks. You might be lucky enough to hear an elusive Black Rail. Good numbers of shorebirds are present when water levels are low, especially during the winter and migration period.

Species of Interest: Tundra Swan, Hooded Merganser, White Ibis, rails, shorebirds

Habitats: maritime forest and shrub, managed waterfowl impoundment, salt marsh

Special Concern: Hunting is allowed on Game Lands during certain times of year (though no hunting is currently allowed on the impoundment at Roanoke Island Marsh Game Land). Birders should be aware of current hunting regulations and seasons and take adequate safety precautions during those times. For more on hunting season safety precautions, see the hunting season information at the beginning of this guide.

Access & Parking: Parking is available at the entrance. An information kiosk provides visitors with interpretive materials and useful site information.

Directions: From Manteo, travel NC 345 south towards Wanchese. At the intersection of US 64/264 continue south on NC 345 for 0.3 miles to the left-hand entrance and parking area.

Coordinates: N 35°53'2" W 75°39'30"
DeLorme (NC Gazetteer) Page: 49

© Nate Bacheler

3

Jockey's Ridge State Park ♿ 🚶 🏕️ 🪑 🚻 ❓ 🔭 🧗

Roanoke Sound

Atlantic Ocean

3

158

catchers, warblers, and sparrows may be seen in the shrub thickets around the base of the dunes. Marked trails leave from the visitor center and head west, toward Roanoke Sound. The sound-side of Jockey's Ridge is home to a variety of wintering waterfowl and can be a good spot from which to raptor-watch during the fall migration.

Species of Interest: American Oystercatcher, migrating raptors, wintering waterfowl

Habitats: maritime forest and shrub, salt marsh, beach and dune

Access & Parking: Parking is available at the visitor center and at the Sound Access Area off Soundside Road. The park is open from 8am to 6pm, November - February; 8am to 7pm, March and October; 8am to 8pm, April, May, and September; 8am to 9pm, June - August. Hang gliding concessions are available.

Directions: The park entrance is at milepost 12 on the US 158 Bypass in Nags Head.

Coordinates: N 37°57'51" W 75°37'57"
DeLorme (NC Gazetteer) Page: 49

Site Information:
Owner: NC State Parks
Milepost 12, US 158 (Croatan Highway),
Nags Head, NC 27595
Dare County
252-441-7132
www.ncsparks.net

About the Site:
Jockey's Ridge State Park is home to the highest sand dune on the east coast. The hot, dry climate of the park yields a unique plant and animal community in this harsh, yet fragile, environment. Though lesser known as a birding destination on the Outer Banks compared to other nearby sites, birding at the park is good in late summer and fall when large numbers of migrating songbirds travel southward. Fly-

Cape Hatteras National Seashore - Bodie Island

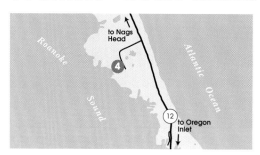

Site Information:
Owner: National Park Service
NC 12, just south of Nags Head, NC
Dare County
252-473-2111
www.nps.gov/caha/bodielh.htm

About the Site:
At the Bodie Island Lighthouse, cross the lawn to the viewing platform by the nearby marsh area. Scan for shorebirds and wading birds. A 0.25 mile long trail leaves from behind the visitor center and connects to a freshwater pond. To view the south side of the pond and adjacent wetlands, take the Bodie Island Dike Trail located on the south of the parking lot; this trail is 0.75 miles in length. Watch for wading birds, Black-necked Stilt, American Avocet, and numerous waterfowl species in winter. Returning to NC 12 on the entry road, and go directly across the road for Coquina Beach. In winter, scan the ocean for loons, Northern Gannet, scoters, and other waterfowl. In spring and fall watch for migrating shorebirds, including Whimbrel, Red Knot, and Black-bellied Plover. In summer, Black Skimmer, Least, Common and Gull-billed Terns are often feeding in the near shore waters. To reach the Bodie Island spit and Oregon Inlet, turn left on Ramp 4 (off-road vehicle ramp) just past the Oregon Inlet Campground and across from the

© Jeff Lewis

Sanderling

Oregon Inlet marina. Two wheel drive vehicles must stop immediately and park along the hard packed side of this unpaved road.

Species of Interest: Black-necked Stilt, American Avocet, Gull-billed Tern, Least Tern, Black Skimmer, wintering waterfowl

Habitats: isolated wetlands, maritime forest and shrub, salt marsh, beach and dune

Special Concern: Hunting is allowed on National Park Service land during certain times of the year. Birders should be aware of current hunting regulations and seasons and take adequate safety precautions during those times. For more on hunting season safety precautions, see the hunting season information at the beginning of this guide. Ask for a brochure with ORV regulations and beach driving tips at any Park Service visitor center.

Access & Parking: The Bodie Island Lighthouse is open daily, 9am to 5pm, September - May; 9am to 6pm, June - August. Birders are encouraged to pick up a park brochure and map from the visitor center. At Oregon Inlet, two-wheel vehicles must park along the hard packed area at the off-road vehicle ramp (Ramp 4). This access area is open daily, year-round.

Directions: All of Bodie Island, just south of Nags Head, is part of the Cape Hatteras National Seashore. From the intersection of US 64/NC 12/US 158 in Nags Head, take NC 12 south for approximately 5.75 miles to the right-hand entrance of the Bodie Island Lighthouse. To reach Oregon Inlet, proceed further south on NC 12, cross the Bonner Bridge and turn left onto the off-road vehicle ramp (Ramp 4) just past the Oregon Inlet Campground and across from the Oregon Inlet Marina. Two wheel vehicles must stop immediately and park along the hard packed side of this unpaved trail.

Coordinates: N 35°49'04" W 75°33'51"
DeLorme (NC Gazetteer) Page: 49

5

© Walker Golder

Pea Island National Wildlife Refuge

♿ 🚶 🚻 ❓ 🔭 🏠

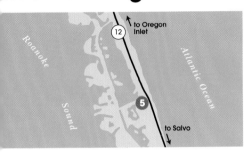

Site Information:
Owner: US Fish and Wildlife Service
NC 12, south of Oregon Inlet on Hatteras Island, NC
Dare County
252-473-1131
www.fws.gov/peaisland/

About the Site:
Pea Island National Wildlife Refuge is one of the finest birding sites in the entire state. More than 5,000 acres in size, the refuge is bordered on the west by Pamlico Sound and on the east by the Atlantic Ocean. Habitats range from salt marsh, to maritime scrub-shrub, to freshwater impoundments, to beach and dune. Spring and fall migrations are prime time to bird at Pea Island. Start out at the visitor center, where a trail leads through a short stretch of maritime forest and along a large impoundment. Watch for a wide variety of shorebirds, including Black Skimmer, Black-necked Stilt, American Avocet, and the occasional rarity, such as the Long-billed Curlew. During winter, thousands of Snow Geese crowd the refuge impoundments, along with Tundra Swan, Gadwall, Northern Pintail, Green-winged Teal and many other waterfowl species. In the marshes just west of the impoundment, listen and watch for a variety of rail species. Piping Plover,

Marsh Wren, Seaside Sparrow, and many wading birds are year round residents. A variety of gulls and terns can also be seen, including Black and Caspian Tern. On the ocean side in late fall and winter, scan the horizon for passing scoters, mergansers, loons, and grebes.

Species of Interest: Snow Goose, Tundra Swan, Horned Grebe, Piping Plover, Black-necked Stilt, American Avocet

Habitats: managed waterfowl impoundments, maritime forest, salt marsh, beach and dune

Special Concern: Hunting is allowed on National Park Service land during certain times of the year. Birders should be aware of current hunting regulations and seasons and take adequate safety precautions during those times. For more on hunting season safety precautions, see the hunting season information at the beginning of this guide. Ask for a brochure with ORV regulations and beach driving tips at any Park Service visitor center.

Access & Parking: Park at the visitor center to access the North Pond impoundment. Inquire at the visitor center about other parking areas from which to access beach and dune habitats and to pick up a refuge map. The visitor center is open daily, 9am to 5pm during the summer and 9am to 4pm year-round. Hours may vary depending on volunteer staffing availability.

Directions: From Nags Head, take NC 12 south. After crossing Bonner Bridge at Oregon Inlet, the visitor center entrance will be approximately 3.75 miles on the right.

Coordinates: N 35°42'58" W 75°29'37"
DeLorme (NC Gazetteer) Page: 49

Outer Banks Group

© Walker Golder

Snow Geese over Pea Island National Wildlife Refuge

© Jeff Lewis

Pileated Woodpeckers

While You're In the Area

Fort Raleigh National Historic Site
National Park Service
1401 National Park Drive
Manteo, North Carolina 27954
252-473-5772
www.nps.gov/fora

Historic Albemarle Tour, Inc.
NC Heritage Trail
PO Box 1604
Washington, NC 27889
800-734-1117
www.historicnenc.com

HomegrownHandmade
Art Roads and Farm Trails of North Carolina
www.homegrownhandmade.com

North Carolina Aquarium at Roanoke Island
374 Airport Road
Manteo, North Carolina 27954-0967
1-866-332-3475
www.ncaquariums.com/ri/riindex.htm

North Carolina Maritime Museum on Roanoke Island
106 Fernando Street
Manteo, NC 27954
252-475-1750
www.ah.dcr.state.nc.us/sections/maritime/branches/roanoke_default.htm

Wright Brothers National Memorial
National Park Service
Mile post 7.5, Highway 158
Kill Devil Hills, NC 27948
252-473-2111
www.nps.gov/wrbr

Welcome to the
Southern Outer Banks Group

The Southern Outer Banks Group offers amazing Outer Banks birding experiences along the lower sections of Cape Hatteras National Seashore. Local birders are familiar with the diverse and abundant numbers of wading birds, waterfowl, shorebirds, gulls, and terns that are possible along the lower reaches of the Outer Banks throughout the year. Summer offers great chances for observing breeding solitary and colonial waterbirds. Superb pelagic birding is waiting in the offshore areas of Cape Hatteras, thanks to the close proximity of Gulf Stream waters.

You Are Here

Raleigh

© John Ennis

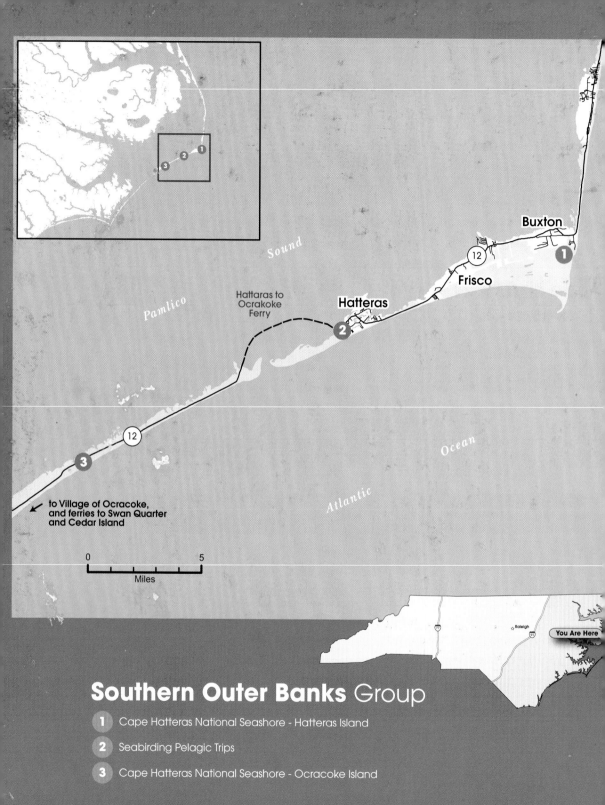

Sound

Pamlico

Hattaras to
Ocrakoke
Ferry

Buxton

12

Frisco

Hatteras

2

1

12

3

Ocean

Atlantic

to Village of Ocracoke,
and ferries to Swan Quarter
and Cedar Island

0   5
Miles

Raleigh

You Are Here

Southern Outer Banks Group

1 Cape Hatteras National Seashore - Hatteras Island

2 Seabirding Pelagic Trips

3 Cape Hatteras National Seashore - Ocracoke Island

© Walker Golder

Gull-billed Tern

Cape Hatteras National Seashore - Hatteras Island

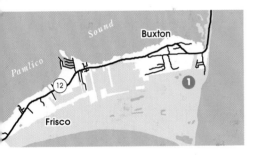

Site Information:
Owner: National Park Service
Cape Hatteras Lighthouse: just beyond
Milepost 61, Buxton, NC
Dare County
252-473-2111
www.nps.gov/caha/capehatteras.htm

About the Site:

Follow the entrance road to the Cape Hatteras Lighthouse toward the Old Lighthouse site; this is a good spot for winter birding. Look for Red-breasted Merganser, scoters, Purple Sandpiper and Bonaparte's Gull. From the lighthouse drive 0.2 miles to the Buxton Woods Nature Trail (a 0.75 mile loop). This wooded area can be very productive during spring and fall migration weather events. Continue to the British Cemetery Trail, a good site for songbirds in spring and fall, and then on to the Ranger Station, toward Cape Point Campground. Among the extensive marshy thickets and vegetation, watch for a wide variety of species - possibilities include Green Heron, Prairie Warbler, Blue Grosbeak. From the campground, continue to the first parking area on the left. The pond to the north hosts wading birds and gulls in summer and diving ducks in winter. The paved road to the left leads to Ramp 43, which gives access to the Salt Pond and Cape Point. Four-wheel drive is needed. Ask for a brochure with ORV regulations and beach driving tips at any Park Service visitor center or check bulletin boards. From the ramp, follow the shoreline south until after the nearest dune, then swing right and slightly uphill to the west to reach Salt Pond. Watch for White and Glossy Ibis feeding in the marshy areas. Look for a variety of waterfowl in Salt Pond, including Tundra Swan, White-winged Scoter, and Lesser Scaup. During summer, watch for Osprey, terns, and herons. From the Salt Pond, cross to the ocean to look for migrating shorebirds as you continue toward the Point. Cape Point offers good opportunities to view winter waterfowl, loons, gannets, grebes and the occasional pelagic species.

Species of Interest: Wilson's Plover, Piping Plover, American Oystercatcher, Gull-billed Tern, Least Tern, wintering waterfowl

Habitats: maritime forest and shrub, salt marsh, beach and dune

(continues)

Special Concerns: Nesting seaturtles and shorebirds are present in the summer time. Please respect the posted areas for nesting birds and turtles. Hunting is allowed on National Park Service land during certain times of the year. Birders should be aware of current hunting regulations and seasons and take adequate safety precautions during those times. For more on hunting season safety precautions, see the hunting season information at the beginning of this guide.

Access & Parking: The Hatteras Island Visitor Center is open daily from 9am to 5pm, September - May; 9am to 6pm, June - August. Visitors are encouraged to pick up a park brochure and map from the Visitor Center. There are many access points for good birding opportunities throughout the park grounds, including the Old Lighthouse Site, the Buxton Woods Nature Trail, the Ranger Station, Cape Point Campground,

the Salt Pond, and Cape Point. All but Cape Point can be accessed by paved roads within the park grounds. Cape Point is accessed on foot (approximately 1 mile each way) or by 4-wheel drive vehicle. Take note of posted beach regulations. Ask for a brochure with ORV regulations and beach driving tips at any Park Service visitor center.

Directions: On Hatteras Island, the Cape Hatteras National Seashore begins in the village of Rodanthe, at Milepost 37 on NC 12. From here, it continues south to Hatteras Inlet, some 35 miles south. Traveling south on NC 12, the entrance to the Cape Hatteras Lighthouse and Visitor Center is just beyond Milepost 61, on the left. This section of the National Seashore provides extensive birding opportunities.

Coordinates: N 35°15'05" W 75°31'38" DeLorme (NC Gazetteer) Page: 69

© Walker Golder

Brown Pelicans in flight

© Nate Bacheler

Wilson's Storm-Petrels

Seabirding Pelagic Trips

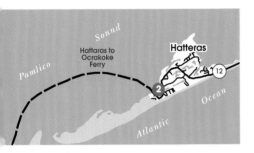

Site Information:
Owner: Brian Patteson
Gulf Stream, offshore
Dare County
252-986-1363
www.seabirding.com

About the Site:

The cool Labrador Current collides with the warm Gulf Stream off the coast of Cape Hatteras, near the edge of the continental shelf, making this area one of the best for viewing seabirds of the western Atlantic Ocean. Offshore trips to view these seabirds leave Hatteras Village early in the morning aboard a local charter boat. Experienced spotters assist birders in locating key species. The best times of year to take such a trip, in terms of species diversity and productivity, are May - September and January - March. In the summer, most trips encounter Black-capped Petrel, Bridled and Sooty Terns, Cory's, Greater and Audubon's Shearwaters, and Band-rumped and Wilson's Storm-Petrels. In May and September, there is also a chance of seeing migrating jaegers, phalaropes and terns. Winter trips can include Northern Fulmar, Manx Shearwater, Great Skua, Black-legged Kittiwake and various alcids.

Species of Interest: Black-capped Petrel, Manx Shearwater, Audubon's Shearwater, Band-rumped Storm-Petrel, White-tailed Tropicbird, alcids

Habitats: nearshore and offshore ocean waters

Special Concerns: Sea conditions may vary; take precautions against seasickness. Dress appropriately for changing weather. In addition to the previously mentioned species, these trips sometimes encounter rare and uncommon visitors such as Herald, Fea's, and Bermuda Petrel, White-faced Storm Petrel, Brown and Masked Booby, White-tailed and Red-billed Tropicbird, and South Polar Skua. In recent years, European Storm-Petrel have been seen on a number of spring trips, and a number of "mega-rarities" have been seen once or twice: Yellow-nosed Albatross, Cape Verde Shearwater, Black-bellied Storm-Petrel, and Swinhoe's Storm Petrel.

Access & Parking: Interested participants must call in advance to make a reservation. Cancellations due to weather will be rescheduled for the following day, if possible. Parking for the trips is available at the Hatteras Landing Marina. Trips usually last from approximately 6am to 5pm.

Directions: From points on the Outer Banks, take NC 12 south to Hatteras Village. In Hatteras, pass by Teach's Lair Marina and take the last right before the Ocracoke Ferry to Hatteras Landing Marina. The boat is usually docked there, though during certain times of the year, it may be elsewhere.

Coordinates: N 35°12'33" W 75°42'06"
DeLorme (NC Gazetteer) Page: 69

Southern Outer Banks Group

77

Cape Hatteras National Seashore - Ocracoke Island

to Village of Ocracoke, and ferries to Swan Quarter and Cedar Island

Site Information:
Owner: National Park Service
Ocracoke Island, NC
Dare County
252-473-2111
www.nps.gov/caha

About the Site:
All of the birding areas within Cape Hatteras National Seashore on Ocracoke Island are off of the primary road that runs the length of the island, NC 12. An ocean-side pond 0.3 miles south of the Hatteras Ferry terminal is a good spot in late fall and winter for viewing water-fowl. The Hammock Hills Nature Trail, across from the National Park Service Campground, is a nice area to watch for wading birds, marsh birds and migrating songbirds. Several park-ing areas along NC 12 offer access to the beach. During the breeding season, Brown Pel-ican, Black Skimmer, and Least, Common and Gull-billed Terns can be seen in the near-shore waters. During spring and fall migration, Red Knots, Sanderling, Black-bellied Plover and other shorebirds can be seen along the surf zone. South Point Road (Ramp 72), just north of Ocracoke Village on the ocean side, is another good birding area. If you're able to access it, South Point Flats, 0.7 miles south of the end of Ramp 72, is a good place to view shore-birds, wading birds and colonial nesting waterbirds. Please respect posted areas to protect the birds.

© Jeff Lewis

Species of Interest: Wilson's Plover, Piping Plover, American Oystercatcher, Least Tern, Gull-billed Tern, Black Skimmer

Habitats: maritime forest and shrub, salt marsh, beach and dune

Special Concerns: Nesting seaturtles and shorebirds are present in the summer time. Please respect the posted areas for nest-ing birds and turtles. Hunting is allowed on National Park Service land during certain times of the year. Birders should be aware of current hunting regulations and seasons and take adequate safety precautions during those times. For more on hunting season safety precautions, see the hunting season information at the beginning of this guide.

Access & Parking: The Ocracoke Visitor Center, located near the ferry terminal in Ocracoke Village, is open daily from 9am to 5pm, September - May; 9am to 6pm, June - August. Visitors are encouraged to pick up a park brochure and map from the Visitor Center. Numerous parking and access areas are designated with signs along NC 12. Four-wheel drive vehicles are recommended and often required for ocean-side vehicle access ramps and sound-side access roads. Ask for a brochure with ORV regulations and beach driving tips at any Park Service visitor center or check bulletin boards. Some sites may be inaccessible during inclement weather due to flooding. Camping (fee) is available at the National Park Service campground on the island; a reservation is required.

Directions: Ocracoke Island can be ac-cessed via car ferry from Hatteras Island (free) or from mainland car ferries (fee required) from Cedar Island or Swan Quarter, NC (reservations are a must during the sum-mer tourist season). Once on the island, NC 12 is the only road that runs the length of the island. All birding sites can be accessed off of NC 12.

Coordinates: N 35°08'04" W 75°54'20"
DeLorme (NC Gazetteer) Page: 69

Southern Outer Banks Group

© Jeff Lewis

Northern Gannets

© Nate Bacheler

The Gulf Stream at sunrise

While You're In the Area

Cape Hatteras Lighthouse
National Park Service
Hwy 12
Buxton, NC 27920
252-473-2111
www.nps.gov/caha/index.htm

Frisco Native American Museum and Natural History Center
Hwy 12
Frisco, NC 27936
252-995-4440
http://nativeamericanmuseum.org/

Historic Albemarle Tour, Inc.
NC Heritage Trail
PO Box 1604
Washington, NC 27889
800-734-1117
www.historicnenc.com

(continues)

A view from the ferry

Piping Plovers

HomegrownHandmade
Art Roads and Farm Trails of North Carolina
www.homegrownhandmade.com

Ocracoke - Cedar Island and
Ocracoke - Swan Quarter Ferries
NC Department of Transportation, Ferry Division
800-345-1665
www.ncdot.org/transit/ferry

Welcome to the
Central Coastal Plain Group

The Central Coastal Plain offers a combination of both urban and rural settings, as well as secluded and public sites. All of the sites on this section of the Trail are situated along two major coastal plain rivers and their tributaries, the Neuse River and the Tar-Pamlico River. These rivers provide important habitat for a variety of birds and offer beautiful settings for birding. Travelers to this area will enjoy diverse birding opportunities and an abundance of historical and cultural attractions in the cities and towns they visit along the way.

You Are Here

☆ Raleigh

© Joseph Peacos, Jr.

Central Coastal Plain Group

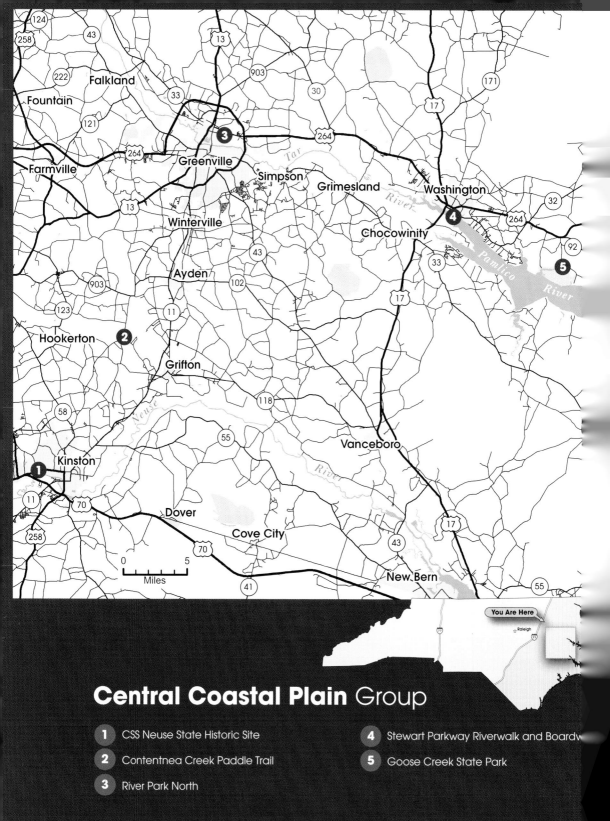

Central Coastal Plain Group

1. CSS Neuse State Historic Site
2. Contentnea Creek Paddle Trail
3. River Park North
4. Stewart Parkway Riverwalk and Boardw[alk]
5. Goose Creek State Park

© Joseph Peacos, Jr.

Great Blue Heron

CSS Neuse State Historic Site

♿ ⛉ 🚻 👤🏠

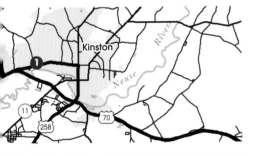

River floodplain, which provides a much larger forested patch within the town of Kinston. Start birding around the parking lot where shrubs and live oaks provide good food and cover for birds. Proceed down the hill toward the picnic area along the Neuse River. Mature hardwoods and river swamp habitats provide good areas for woodpeckers, flycatchers and vireos.

Species of Interest: Great Crested Flycatcher, Brown Creeper, wading birds

Habitats: floodplain forest, river

Access & Parking: Normal hours of operation are 10am to 5pm, Monday - Friday. Visitors are encouraged to call ahead, as hours sometimes vary throughout the year.

Directions: From US 70, west of downtown Kinston, exit on US 70 Business East (West Vernon Avenue). The site entrance is approximately 0.5 miles on the right.

Coordinates: N 35°16'00" W 77°37'17" DeLorme (NC Gazetteer) Page: 64

Site Information:
Owner: NC Department of Cultural Resources
2612 West Vernon Avenue, Kinston, NC 28504
Lenoir County
252-522-2091
www.cssneuse.nchistoricsites.org

About the Site:
This State Historic Site houses the remains of the CSS Neuse, a confederate ironclad gunboat. Guided tours of the ship's remains are available. Even if you don't plan to tour the CSS Neuse, the site is worth a stop for birding if you're in the area. Although the site is only 46 acres in size, it backs up against the Neuse

(2)

Contentnea Creek Paddle Trail

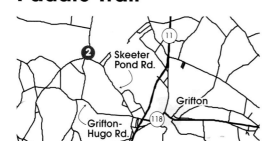

Site Information:
Owner: Greene County
Edward's Bridge to Grifton, NC
Greene/Lenoir/Pitt County line
252-747-3446
www.ncsu.edu/paddletrails/

About the Site:

This site is part of the Lower Neuse Bottom-lands Important Bird Area, as designated by Audubon NC. This 9.5 mile stretch of Contentnea Creek is a good section for birding. At the Edward's Bridge put-in, the creek is approximately 30 yards wide, which makes it easy to see and hear birds on both sides of the creek. It's also wide enough so fallen trees don't block the entire width of the creek, so no portaging is necessary. The creek is rather slow and muddy during most flows. It can be a little difficult to observe birds through binoculars, even while floating at a slow pace, so most birding will be done by ear. Still, birders should have no trouble listing over 50 species for the trip. Watch for Red-shouldered Hawk overhead, and listen for Acadian Flycatcher, Yellow-throated Vireo, Northern Parula, Prothonotary Warbler and other songbirds. Belted Kingfisher nest on the banks of the creek. Muskrats, beavers and numerous snakes and turtles are also common.

Species of Interest: Great Crested Flycatcher, Prothonotary Warbler, American Redstart

Habitats: pine/hardwood forest, floodplain forest, creek

Access & Parking: The trail put-in is at Edwards Bridge on Hugo Road (SR 1004); the take-out is at the NC Wildlife Resources Commission boat ramp in Grifton. Limited parking is available at the Edwards Bridge site. Parking is available at the Grifton boat access, though paddlers should give parking preference to boat trailers. The paddle trail may be accessed during daylight hours, year round. Contact the Pamlico-Tar River Foundation at (252) 946-7211, info@ptrf.org, for a copy of the Pitt County Paddle Trails brochure, which contains a map of the Contentnea Creek Paddle Trail.

Directions: To the Grifton boat ramp: from downtown Grifton turn east on NC 118. Travel 0.4 miles and turn right on Martin Luther King Jr. Drive. After one block, Martin Luther King Jr. Drive turns into Waters Street. The NC Wildlife Resources Commission boat access is on the left.

From the take-out in Grifton to the put-in at Edwards Bridge: from the Grifton boat ramp, take Waters Street/Martin Luther King Jr. Drive back to NC 118. Turn left on NC 118 West. Go 0.4 miles and turn left on South Highland Blvd. After the John E. Cameron bridge, turn right on Contentnea Road. Cross NC 11, where the road becomes Grifton-Hugo Road, and turn right on Skeeter Pond Road (SR 1709). Travel for 3.4 miles and turn right on Hugo Road (SR 1004). The boat ramp is 0.3 miles along Hugo Road, immediately after the bridge crossing, on the left.

Coordinates: N 35°24'48" W 77°29'52"
DeLorme (NC Gazetteer) Page: 65

© Joseph Peacos, Jr.

Anhinga

River Park North

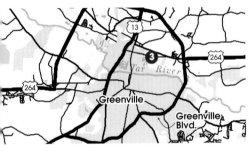

Site Information:
Owner: City of Greenville
1000 Mumford Road, Greenville, NC 27858
Pitt County
252-329-4560
www.greenvillenc.gov

About the Site:

River Park North is a 324-acre park along the Tar River, most of which is rich bottomland forest. The park also contains fields and open areas, and numerous small lakes. Several trails through the property offer excellent birding opportunities. The main trail leading south from the parking area passes by three small lakes before entering a wooded area for a short distance. Watch for Bald Eagle and Osprey overhead and look for waterfowl, grebes and wading birds at the lakes. In the wooded areas, listen for Prothonotary Warbler, Northern Parula, and other birds of moist woodlands. The trail then passes by a power line right-of-way where early successional species such as

Common Yellowthroat, Indigo Bunting and Blue Grosbeak may be heard and seen. Finally, the trail enters a cypress swamp forest as it heads toward the river (portions of this section may be closed due to seasonal flooding). The Greenville-River Park North Birding Club maintains a bird list for the property. Inquire at the visitor center for the list.

Species of Interest: Anhinga, Bald Eagle, Prothonotary Warbler, Indigo Bunting, Blue Grosbeak, wintering waterfowl

Habitats: pine/hardwood forest, floodplain forest, early successional, lakes

Access & Parking: An informational kiosk with a map is located near the parking area. Numerous trails leave from the open area just south of the parking area. River Park North is open 6am to 8pm, Tuesday - Sunday (seasonal hours may vary so call ahead). Primitive camping is available by advanced reservation.

Directions: From Memorial Drive (NC 13/11/903) by the Pitt/Greenville Airport, turn east on Airport Road, which turns into Mumford Road in approximately 0.3 miles. The park is located 0.75 miles down Mumford Road on the right. Signs mark the entrance prominently.

Coordinates: N 35°37'43" W 77°21'37"
DeLorme (NC Gazetteer) Page: 43

85

Stewart Parkway Riverwalk and Boardwalk

$ ♿ 🚶 🚻 ? 🔭 🏠

Site Information:

Contact: NC Estuarium
223 East Water Street, Washington, NC 27889
Beaufort County
252-948-0000
www.partnershipforthesounds.org/nce_home.htm

About the Site:

The Stewart Parkway Riverwalk is a brick promenade that connects to a wooden boardwalk beginning at the NC Estuarium. The boardwalk extends east along the Pamlico River, past manmade wetlands with views of nearby Castle Island on the river. A variety of wetland associated species can be seen from the boardwalk, depending on the season. Watch for rafts of waterfowl and grebes in wintertime. In the spring and summer, watch for osprey, terns, herons, and egrets. Bald Eagle may be spotted year round. An Anhinga is a very rare possibility.

Species of Interest: Red-breasted Merganser, Bald Eagle, Least Tern, wading birds

Habitats: river, isolated wetlands

Access & Parking: Roadside parking is available around the Estuarium and along Stewart Parkway. The boardwalk is free and can be accessed year round during daylight hours. The Estuarium charges an admission fee ($3/adult and $2/student). The facilities are open 10am to 4pm, Tuesday - Saturday. The Estuarium leads interpretive nature programs; inquire within about availability or check website.

Directions: From US 17, turn east on Main Street (one block north of the Pamlico River) and then make a quick right on Stewart Parkway. Travel for 3 blocks until Stewart Parkway enters Water Street. The Estuarium is located at 223 East Water Street.

Coordinates: N 35°32'23" W 77°03'14"
DeLorme (NC Gazetteer) Page: 66

© Walker Golder

Northern Shovelers.

Central Coastal Plain Group

86

Goose Creek State Park

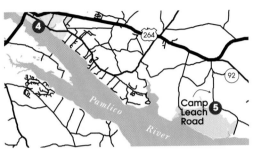

Site Information:
Owner: NC State Parks
2190 Camp Leach Road, Washington, NC 27889
Beaufort County
252-923-2191
www.ncsparks.net

About the Site:

Goose Creek State Park is a haven for birds. Access to a variety of habitats, from brackish marsh and freshwater swamps, to open fields and mature mixed forest, provides birders with opportunities to view a wide variety of birds in all seasons. Boardwalks provide up-close encounters with nesting Prothonotary Warbler and other wetland birds. Barred Owl and Red-shouldered Hawk reside in the wooded swamps. A feeder station provides an easy way to view locally common species, such as Brown-headed Nuthatch. Trails in upland mixed forest are abundant with Red-headed Woodpecker, Summer Tanager, and flycatchers in the breed-

Northern Parula

ing season. Golden-crowned Kinglet flit in the tree-tops in winter. View nesting Osprey along the marshy creeks and rivers in the warmer months, or look for wintering waterfowl such as Lesser Scaup, Common Goldeneye or Red-breasted Merganser in the cooler months. Keep your eyes to the sky and you may catch a glimpse of a Bald Eagle at any time of year.

Birders at Goose Creek State Park

Species of Interest: Bald Eagle, Red-headed Woodpecker, Brown-headed Nuthatch, Prothonotary Warbler, Summer Tanager, wintering waterfowl

Habitats: pine/hardwood forest, coastal swampland, brackish and freshwater marsh

Access & Parking: Parking is available at the main visitor center and throughout the park. The park is open from 8am to 6pm, November - February; 8am to 7pm, March and October; 8am to 8pm, April, May, and September; 8am to 9pm, June - August. The visitor center is open daily, 8am to 4:30pm.

Directions: From Washington, follow US 264 east for 10 miles to Camp Leach Road (SR 1334). Turn right and travel 2.25 miles to the park entrance on the right.

Coordinates: N 35°28'42" W 76°54'09"
DeLorme (NC Gazetteer) Page: 66

Central Coastal Plain Group

©Jeff Lewis

Carolina Chickadee

River Park North

©David Allen

While You're In the Area

Historic Albemarle Tour, Inc.
NC Heritage Trail
PO Box 1604
Washington, NC 27889
800-734-1117
www.historicnenc.com

HomegrownHandmade
Art Roads and Farm Trails of North Carolina
www.homegrownhandmade.com

Neuseway Nature Park, Planetarium, Health & Science Museum
401 W Caswell Street
Kinston, NC 27925
252-939-3367
www.neusewaypark.com

Wilson Botanical Gardens
1806 S.W. Goldsboro Street
Wilson, NC 27893
252-237-0113
www.wilson-co.com/arboretum.html

Welcome to the
Western Coastal Plain Group

T he Western Coastal Plain offers a chance for visitors to experience the heart of eastern North Carolina and the people and places the area is home to. Travel the back roads that cross Johnston, Sampson, Duplin, and Wayne counties to explore four very unique sites. Each offers equally distinctive birding opportunities, and welcoming communities. You'll be glad you took the time to experience this rural portion of the coastal plain Trail.

You Are Here

Raleigh

© NC State Parks

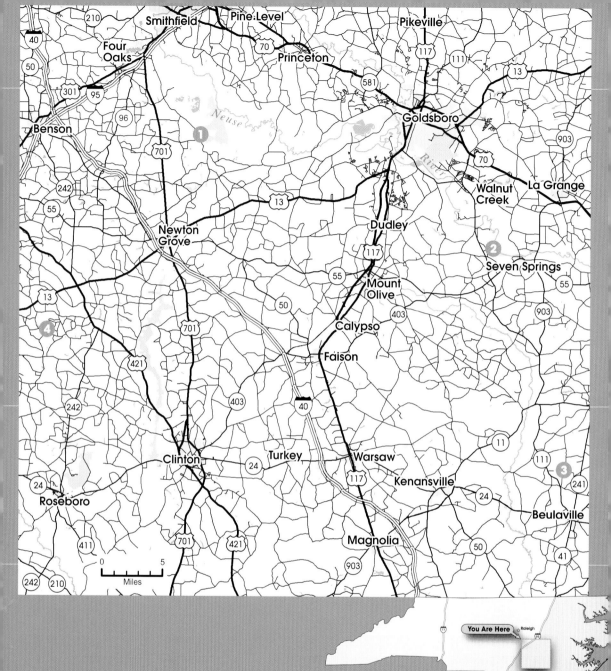

Western Coastal Plain Group

1 Howell Woods Environmental Learning Center

2 Cliffs of the Neuse State Park

3 Cabin Lake County Park

4 Jackson Farm

Howell Woods
Environmental Learning Center

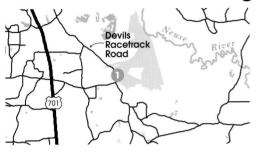

Devils
Racetrack
Road

Neuse
River

701

Site Information:
Owner: Johnston Community College
6601 Devils Racetrack Road,
Four Oaks, NC 27524
Johnston County
919-938-0115
www.johnstoncc.edu/howellwoods

About the Site:
More than 170 species of birds have been documented at this unique 2,856 acre property that is actively managed for the benefit of wildlife, conservation education and outdoor recreation. There are more than 25 miles of unpaved roads and trails and the site is dominated by over 1,600 acres of bottomland forest along the Neuse River. In addition, there are longleaf pine woodlands, a variety of mixed hardwood/pine forests and abundant early successional habitats with good birding year-round. Breeding species include Mississippi Kite, Red-headed Woodpecker, Brown-headed Nuthatch, a variety of wood warblers, Summer Tanager and

Orchard Oriole, among others. Winter birding is also excellent, with abundant sparrows, raptors and even some waterfowl present on some of the small ponds. Most anytime of year will yield high bird counts, especially during spring and fall migration.

Species of Interest: Mississippi Kite, Loggerhead Shrike, Prothonotary Warbler, Swainson's Warbler, Kentucky Warbler, Hooded Warbler

Habitats: pine/hardwood forest, floodplain forest, longleaf pine forest, early successional

Special Concern: Hunting is allowed at Howell Woods during certain times of year. Birders should be aware of current hunting regulations and seasons and take adequate safety precautions during those times. For more on hunting season safety precautions, see the hunting season information at the beginning of this guide.

Access & Parking: Office hours are 8am to 5pm, Monday - Friday. Most trails on the property are open 7 days a week during daylight hours. Certain areas may be closed during organized hunts. All visitors should check in at the office before touring the site.

Directions: From Interstate 95, take exit 90 (US 701/NC 96). From I-95 north, turn right from the exit ramp and go over the bridge and turn left onto Devils Racetrack Road (SR 1009) just before the Citgo and BP gas stations. From I-95 south, turn left onto NC 96 and then almost immediately cross US 701 (at the Citgo and BP gas stations) onto Devils Racetrack Road (SR 1009). Travel for 8.25 miles on Devils Racetrack Road and the Learning Center entrance is located on the left. Follow the longleaf pine and wax myrtle lined drive into the parking lot.

Coordinates: N 35°22'14" W 78°18'21"
DeLorme (NC Gazetteer) Page: 63

Loggerhead Shrike

Cliffs of the Neuse State Park ▲ ♿ 🚶 🏕 ⛽ 🚻 ❓ 🏠

Site Information:
Owner: NC State Parks
345-A Park Entrance Road,
Seven Springs, NC 28578
Wayne County
919-778-6234
www.ncsparks.net

About the Site:

Cliffs of the Neuse State Park presents the birder with a unique opportunity to explore a variety of habitats in one distinct location, including a pine forest similar to those in the Sandhills region, an adjacent oak/hickory forest more often associated with the piedmont, and a nearby cypress swamp. The presence of Spanish moss also demonstrates the biological diversity of the park. Though common in the eastern parts of the state, Spanish moss reaches the western limits of its distribution at Cliffs of the Neuse. Birds are an easy study in the park during any season and in any habitat. Four hiking trails are accessible from the museum parking lot. Each is less than a mile in length

River overlook at Cliffs of the Neuse State Park

and offers a closer look into the heart of Cliffs of the Neuse State Park. In late spring, listen for Northern Parula and Prothonotary Warbler along the river. Pine Warbler and Red-headed Woodpecker can be found in the dry pine forest. At dawn or dusk, listen for the song of the Chuck-will's-widow. Fall and winter bring a host of migratory waterfowl to the area to join the native Wood Duck.

Species of Interest: Chuck-will's-widow, Red-headed Woodpecker, Prothonotary Warbler

Habitats: pine/hardwood forest, floodplain forest, river

Special Feature: The Cliffs of the Neuse are a spectacular series of cliffs extending for 600 yards and rising some 90 feet above the water. Layers of sand, clay, seashells, shale and gravel form the multicolored cliff face. The cliffs were formed when a fault in the earth's crust shifted millions of years ago. The Neuse River followed this fault line and, over time, cut its course through layers of sediment deposited by shallow seas that had earlier covered the coastal plain. A portion of the river took a bend against its bank and the water's erosive action slowly carved Cliffs of the Neuse.

Access & Parking: The park is open from 8am to 6pm, November - February; 8am to 7pm, March and October; 8am to 8pm, April, May, and September; 8am to 9pm, June - August. The Park Office is open 8am to 5pm, weekdays. Seasonal concessions are available Memorial Day through Labor Day. An interpretive museum is located adjacent to the amphitheater.

Directions: From Goldsboro, take US 70 East to NC 111 South. Travel approximately 9 miles on NC 111 to the park entrance on the left.

Coordinates: N 35°14'23" W 77°53'05"
DeLorme (NC Gazetteer) Page: 64

Cabin Lake County Park

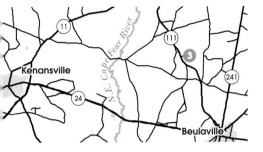

Site Information:
Owner: Duplin County
220 Cabin Lake Road, Pink Hill, NC 28572
Duplin County
910-298-3648
www.duplincountync.com/governmentOffices/parksRecreation.html

About the Site:
Cabin Lake County Park is a beautiful and under-utilized park. Start at one of several parking areas just past the park entrance and walk southeast to the start of the hiking trail. It begins by crossing the dam for the 70 acre lake. Between mowing cycles, as the vegetation on the dam gets a little taller you'll find good sparrow habitat. Look for Savannah and White-throated Sparrows in winter. Proceed around the lake for a 2.2 mile walk. The trail dips in and out of the woods, but never strays far from the lake. Numerous wooden piers allow for good viewing platforms to see wintering waterfowl. As you cross the wooden bridge at the northern corner of the lake, look for Belted Kingfishers nesting in the banks of one of the several islands. Some of the best birding is near the end of the trail as it passes by the camping area. Here the forest canopy is more broken and allows for more forest structure. Look and listen for Brown-headed Nuthatch, Kentucky Warbler, Summer Tanager, and Blue Grosbeak.

Species of Interest: Brown-headed Nuthatch, Kentucky Warbler, Summer Tanager, Blue Grosbeak, winter sparrows, winter waterfowl

Habitats: pine/hardwood forest, lake, early successional

Access & Parking: Admission is $3 per person; ages 5 and under are free. Hours of operation are November - February: 8am to 6pm, Friday - Sunday; March and October: 8am to 7pm, Thursday - Sunday; April - September: 8am to 8pm, Thursday - Sunday. Open Memorial Day, July 4th, and Labor Day. Hours may change seasonally, so it is suggested that visitors call ahead to confirm. Canoe and paddle boat rentals are available. Additional fees apply for use of boat launch and camp sites.

Directions: From Beaulaville, take NC 111 north for 4.5 miles to the park entrance on the right.

Coordinates: N 34°58'51" W 77°47'58"
DeLorme (NC Gazetteer) Page: 76

© Harry Sell

Kentucky Warbler

Western Coastal Plain Group

Jackson Farm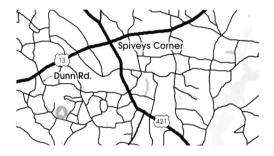

Site Information:
Owners: Tom and Jan Jackson
13902 Dunn Road, Godwin, NC 28344
Sampson County
910-567-2978
www.jacksonfarm.com

© NCDPR - Sean McElhone

Belted Kingfisher

About the Site:

Jackson Farm offers two 1-mile birding trails, each winding through a diversity of upland and lowland habitats. The public birding trail, an easy-to-walk loop suitable for a short visit, begins at Dunn Road and traverses a cropland/forest edge and an early successional shrub wetland. In the summer, birders should expect Northern Bobwhite, Red-headed Woodpecker, Blue Grosbeak and Indigo Bunting along this trail. The early successional habitat is a great place to see Swamp, Fox, and White-throated Sparrow in the winter. The guest house trail, open only to overnight residents of the guest house, bisects 10-acres of mature bottomland forest and upland longleaf pine forest. A pond at the trail head is home to a family of Belted Kingfisher and harbors Canada Goose, Wood Duck and other waterfowl in the winter months. Birders should expect to see Eastern Wood-Pewee, Brown-headed Nuthatch, Pileated Woodpecker, and Prothonotary Warbler along this 1-mile trail. Over the past 20 years, the Jackson's have identified about 100 bird species on their farm.

Species of Interest: Red-headed Woodpecker, Brown-headed Nuthatch, Prothonotary Warbler, Blue Grosbeak, Indigo Bunting, winter sparrows

Habitats: pine/hardwood forest, longleaf pine forest, early successional, moist shrubland

Special Features: Hand-made pottery, potted native plants attractive to wildlife, and bird houses and feeders are sold at the farm. A guesthouse is available for overnight or extended rental.

Access & Parking: Vehicles are not allowed on trails, but a small parking area is available off Dunn Road. The guest house bird trail is open only to birders who rent the guest house. Call or email for guest house reservation.

Directions: From Dunn, drive east on NC 421. Turn right at Spivey's Corner on US 13 and travel for 4 miles. Turn left on Dunn Road (SR 1002) and travel for 3.5 miles, making sure to stay on Dunn Road as it makes a 90 degree right turn. Jackson Farm is on the left at 13902 Dunn Road.

Coordinates: N 35°07'53" W 78°32'35"
DeLorme (NC Gazetteer) Page: 62

© Harry Sell

Baltimore Oriole

While You're In the Area

Bentonville Battlefield
North Carolina Historic Sites
5466 Harper House Road
Four Oaks, NC 27524
910-594-0789
www.ah.dcr.state.nc.us/sections/hs/ben-tonvi/bentonvi.htm

HomegrownHandmade
Art Roads and Farm Trails of North Carolina
www.homegrownhandmade.com

Western Coastal Plain Group

95

Red-breasted Nuthatch

Welcome to the
Lower Neuse Group

The Lower Neuse Group includes a wonderful set of sites that offer impressive birding opportunities. Visitors can explore two vastly different sections of the Croatan National Forest, take a ferry ride across the lower Neuse River as it widens toward the Pamlico Sound, and discover the rural and unspoiled beauty of the Pamlico Peninsula. A visit to Weyerhaeuser's Cool Springs Environmental Education Center provides up-close encounters with both floodplain and managed pine forest bird species.

Raleigh

You Are Here

© Nate Bacheler

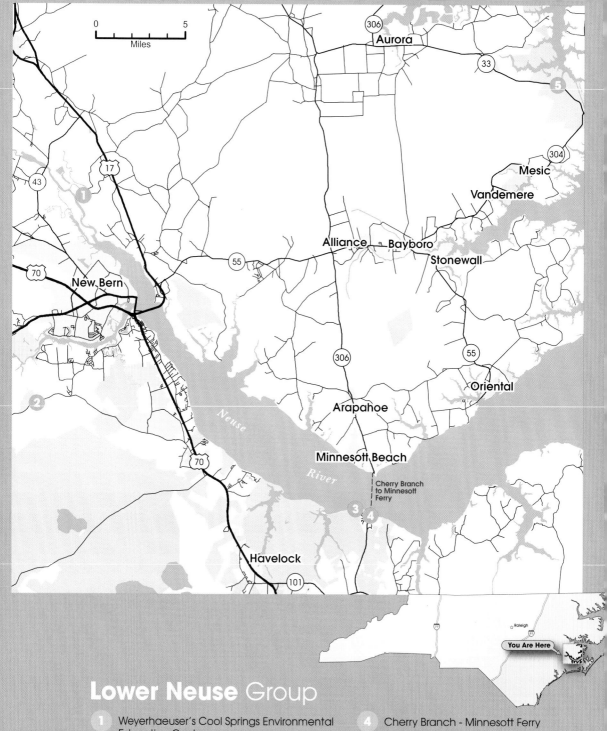

Lower Neuse Group

1. Weyerhaeuser's Cool Springs Environmental Education Center

2. Croatan National Forest - Island Creek Forest Walk

3. Croatan National Forest - Neusiok Trail

4. Cherry Branch - Minnesott Ferry

5. Goose Creek Game Land - Spring Creek Impoundment

Weyerhaeuser's Cool Springs Environmental Education Center

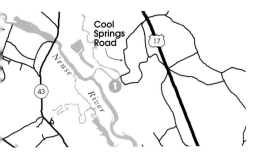

Site Information:
Owner: Weyerhaeuser Company
945 Cool Springs Road, Askin, NC 28527
Craven County
252-633-7017
www.coolsprings.org

About the Site:

Weyerhaeuser's Cool Springs Environmental Education Center is actively managed as a working forest to demonstrate forestry practices, while maintaining and enhancing wildlife habitat, air quality, water quality, as well as aesthetic, recreational and historical values. The site is a great birding spot due to a wide variety of available habitat types. A boardwalk across a swamp forest allows for opportunities to see Prothonotary Warbler, Northern Parula and wading birds. Birders can also expect to see Red-headed Woodpecker, Brown-headed Nuthatch, Hooded Warbler, Summer Tanager, and Indigo Bunting. Visitation for groups is by appointment only. Birding walks of any length can be arranged with the site manager, who will lead visitors through pine stands, upland hardwood forest, wetland forest and early successional habitats. Red-shouldered Hawk, Osprey, Great Crested Flycatcher, Swainson's Warbler, and Blue Grosbeak are other possibilities on-site.

Species of Interest: Great Crested Flycatcher, Brown-headed Nuthatch, Prothonotary Warbler, Swainson's Warbler, Hooded Warbler, Summer Tanager

Habitats: pine/hardwood forest, floodplain forest, longleaf pine forest, early successional

Special Concerns: Mosquitoes, ticks and deer flies can be pesky in warm months. This site allows hunting during late fall and early winter. Birders should be aware of current hunting regulations and seasons and take adequate safety precautions during those times. For more on hunting season safety precautions, see the hunting season information at the beginning of this guide.

Access & Parking: Cool Springs is open year-round, but is available by appointment only. Please call ahead to schedule your visit. Guided tours are available for large groups. Parking is available near the building on-site. The site trails and boardwalk can be accessed from this location. The longleaf pine forest is a short drive from the parking area, and can be explored with the site manager.

Directions: From New Bern, take US 17 north, crossing the Neuse River. Continue on US 17 for approximately 8 miles. Turn left on Askin Brick Road, then another left onto Cool Springs Road. Stay on this road for 2.6 miles to the Cool Springs entrance, marked with a sign. Drive down the entrance road for about 0.5 miles to the picnic shelters and red house. The site manager will meet you there.

Coordinates: N 35°11'21" W 77°05'10"
DeLorme (NC Gazetteer) Page: 66

© John Ennis

Prothonotary Warbler

Lower Neuse Group

Croatan National Forest -  Island Creek Forest Walk

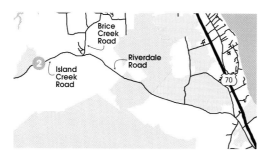

Site Information:
Owner: USDA Forest Service
Island Creek Road, east of Pollocksville, NC
Jones County
252-638-5628
www.cs.unca.edu/nfsnc/recreation/cro-atan.pdf

About the Site:

This is a short hike within mature hardwood and pine habitats along Island Creek, on the outskirts of the Croatan National Forest. The loop trail is less than 1 mile in length, but the bird species diversity is high due to the old growth characteristics on site. Typical breeding songbirds include Yellow-throated Vireo, Wood Thrush, Ovenbird, and Summer Tanager along the uplands, and Acadian Flycatcher, Northern Parula and Louisiana Waterthrush along the creek. Hooded Warbler and Kentucky Warbler are also possible. Migration brings Black-throated Blue Warbler and Scarlet Tanager. In winter look for Brown Creeper and Winter Wren. Occasionally, Purple Finch and Pine Siskin can also be seen in winter. The area supports many plant species that are more typical of the piedmont and mountains of North Carolina. Along the creek are

© Jeff Lewis

Pine Warbler

outcrops of coquina limestone, which make this a very rich site and adds to the plant and bird diversity.

Species of Interest: Great Crested Fly-catcher, Brown-headed Nuthatch, Protho-notary Warbler, Kentucky Warbler, Hooded Warbler, Summer Tanager

Habitats: pine/hardwood forest, floodplain forest

Special Concerns: The trail is not particularly well marked, but it is well worn, so stay on the well worn portion of the trail to avoid getting lost. Poison ivy is plentiful, and mosquitoes can be very bad after wet periods. Hunting is allowed in Croatan National Forest during certain times of the year. Birders should be aware of current hunting regulations and seasons and take adequate safety precautions during those times. For more on hunting season safety precautions, see the hunting season information at the beginning of this guide.

Access & Parking: The access area has parking for approximately 10 cars. The trail is open during daylight hours, year-round. Self-guided brochures can be picked up at the Croatan National Forest District Office, located on US 70, approximately 8 miles south of New Bern.

Directions: From New Bern, travel south/east on US 70. Just beyond the Trent or Neuse River bridge, turn right at the first traffic light onto Williams Road (look for the Burger King on the corner) and reset the odometer. At 1.4 miles, Williams Road ends at Madam Moores Lane. Turn left on Madam Moores Lane, which changes names to Brice Creek Road, then to Island Creek Road. The Island Creek Forest Walk access area is on the right at 8.4 miles. From Pollocksville, the access area is 5.6 miles east of NC 17 on Island Creek Road.

Coordinates: N 35°01'37" W 77°08'10"
DeLorme (NC Gazetteer) Page: 77

Croatan National Forest -  Neusiok Trail

Croatan National Forest

Site Information:
Owner: USDA Forest Service
Northern terminus of trail on Forest Service Road 132 (Pine Cliff Recreation Area), off NC 306, east of Havelock, NC
Craven and Carteret County
252-638-5628
www.cs.unca.edu/nfsnc/recreation/cro-atan.pdf

About the Site:

The Neusiok Trail is a 26 mile long trail that extends from the Neuse River south to the Newport River estuary. Habitats along the way vary from salt marsh, to longleaf pine savanna, to upland hardwood stands, to dense shrub-lands. The trail crosses several paved and un-paved roads. The best birding is typically during the early breeding season, from April-June, and winter. In winter, watch for rafts of diving ducks along the Neuse River as it parallels the northern section of the trail, including Lesser Scaup, Ruddy Duck, Canvasback and Surf Scoter. The Newport River estuary, adjacent to the southern end of the trail, hosts a variety of salt marsh birds; low tide presents the best viewing opportunities. Two recommended sections of the trail for a variety of migrating and breeding songbirds are the section that extends from the NC 306 crossing north to the Neuse River, and the section that extends from NC 101 south to Forest Service Road 147. Listen for Yellow-billed Cuckoo, Eastern Wood-Pe-wee, Great Crested Flycatcher, Brown-headed Nuthatch, Yellow-throated and Pine Warbler,

and Summer Tanager in the upland and slope areas. In wetter areas, Prothonotary Warbler, Northern Parula and Acadian Flycatcher are possibilities.

Species of Interest: Brown-headed Nuthatch, Prothonotary Warbler, Summer Tanager, shorebirds, wading birds, winter waterfowl

Habitats: pine/hardwood forest, longleaf pine forest, floodplain forest, salt marsh

Special Concerns: Some sections of the trail can be very wet. Plan to get your feet wet. During warmer months, plan for heat, insects, and snakes. Hunting is allowed within the Croatan National Forest during certain times of the year. Birders should be aware of current hunting regulations and seasons and take adequate safety precautions during those times. For more on hunting season safety precautions, see the hunting season information at the beginning of this guide.

Access & Parking: Overnight parking is available at both ends of the trail and at the NC 306 crossing, 1.9 miles north of the NC 101/NC 306 intersection. Another crossing, approximately 1 mile east of NC 306 on NC 101, is a good short-term pick-up/drop-off area. There are 3 primitive camping shelters along the trail, where overnight camping is permitted. Information and maps can be picked up at the Croatan National Forest District Office, located on US 70, approximately 8 miles south of New Bern.

(continues)

Lower Neuse Group

Directions: To northern terminus: from NC 101 east of Havelock, turn north on NC 306 (watch for signs to the Cherry Branch-Minnesott Ferry). Go 3.25 miles and turn left on Forest Service Road 132 to reach the Pine Cliff Recreation Area, where the trail begins.

To the southern terminus: From the NC 101/ NC 306 intersection, continue east on NC 101, past the small community of Harlowe.

Turn right on Old Winberry Road (SR 1155) and travel for 3.75 miles. At the intersection of Mill Creek Road (SR 1154) turn right, then make a quick left onto Forest Service Road 181 to reach the Oyster Point campground, the southern terminus of the trail.

Coordinates: N 34°56'19" W 76°49'18"
DeLorme (NC Gazetteer) Page: 78

Cherry Branch - Minnesott Ferry

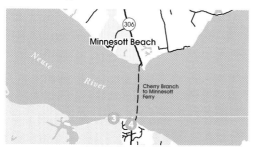

Horned Grebe

Site Information:
Owner: NC Department of Transportation
NC 306 at Neuse River crossing, east of Havelock, NC
Craven and Pamlico County
252-447-1055
www.ncdot.org/transit/ferry

About the Site:

This 20 minute ferry crossing of the Neuse River offers waterfowl and wading bird viewing opportunities. Winter is perhaps the best season for a visit. Regardless of season, the ferry is also a convenient way to simply travel from Pamlico County to Craven or Carteret counties (or visa versa). During winter, watch for Red-breasted Merganser, Common Loon, Horned Grebe, Lesser Scaup, Bufflehead, and a variety of gulls and other wintering waterfowl. In warmer months, be on the lookout for Brown Pelican and terns. The loading areas at either end of the ferry also afford some land-based birding opportunities, though mostly for commonly seen species.

Species of Interest: Canvasback, Horned Grebe, winter waterfowl, wading birds

Habitats: riverine

Access & Parking: The Cherry Branch - Minnesott ferry operates daily from 5:45am to midnight, at 30 minute intervals. Review a current North Carolina Ferry System Schedule to confirm the schedule. This ferry ride is free for passengers and their vehicles.

Directions: In Craven County: from the intersection of US 70 and NC 101 in Havelock, take NC 101 east for 5.2 miles. Turn north on NC 306 and travel 4.4 miles to the ferry dock.

In Pamlico County: from the intersection of NC 306 and NC 55, north of Arapahoe, take NC 306 south for 12 miles to the ferry dock in Minnesott Beach.

Coordinates: N 34°56'06" W 76°48'40" (Craven County side)
DeLorme (NC Gazetteer) Page: 78

Lower Neuse Group

5

Goose Creek Game Land - Spring Creek Impoundment

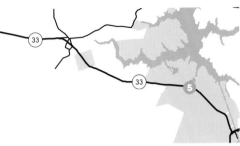

Lower Neuse Group

Site Information:
Owner: NC Wildlife Resources Commission
NC 33, east of Aurora, NC
Beaufort/Pamlico County line
252-514-4737
www.ncwildlife.org

About the Site:

Walk the short trail that leaves from the north side of the parking area. Listen and look for a variety of bird species in the marshes on both sides of the trail, including Osprey, Common Yellowthroat, Red-winged Blackbird and other wetland-associated species. Watch for Bald Eagle overhead. Clapper Rail and other wading birds are probable here; the Black Rail is a rare possibility. Listen for Chuck-will's-widow at dawn or dusk. American Black Duck may be found nesting in the marsh. During the winter, rafts of wintering waterfowl can be spotted on the impoundment. During migration, look for a variety of shorebirds.

Species of Interest: Bald Eagle, Chuck-will's-widow, Red-headed Woodpecker, rails, winter waterfowl, wading birds

Habitats: isolated wetlands, wetland forest, managed waterfowl impoundment

Special Concern: Hunting is allowed on Game Lands during certain times of year. Birders should be aware of current hunting regulations and seasons and take adequate safety precautions during those times. For more on hunting season safety precautions, see the hunting season information at the beginning of this guide.

Access & Parking: A short trail leaves from the parking area and heads north for less than 0.25 miles, to the southwest corner of Spring Creek Impoundment.

Directions: From the intersection of NC 33 and NC 306 in Aurora, head east on NC 33 for 10 miles. After passing the NC Wildlife Resources Commission's Smith Creek Boat Access area, travel 0.8 miles farther and watch for a parking area on the left, signed with a brown and white binoculars sign, indicating a wildlife viewing area.

Coordinates: N 35°16'02" W 76°37'02"
DeLorme (NC Gazetteer) Page: 67

© Brady Beck
Chuck-will's-widow

Boardwalk along the Neusiok Trail

While You're In the Area

Aurora - Bayview Ferry
NC Department of Transportation,
Ferry Division
252-964-4521
www.ncdot.org/transit/ferry

Aurora Fossil Museum
400 Main Street
Aurora, NC 27806-0352
252-322-4238
www.aurorafossilmuseum.com

Cherry Branch - Minnesott Ferry
NC Department of Transportation,
Ferry Division
800-339-9156
www.ncdot.org/transit/ferry

Historic Albemarle Tour, Inc.
NC Heritage Trail
PO Box 1604
Washington, NC 27889
800-734-1117
www.historicnenc.com

HomegrownHandmade
Art Roads and Farm Trails of North Carolina
www.homegrownhandmade.com

Tryon Palace Historic Sites & Gardens
NC Department of Cultural Resources
610 Pollock Street
New Bern, NC 28560
800-767-1560
www.tryonpalace.org

Lower Neuse Group

Welcome to the
East Carteret Group

Carteret County is host to a diversity of coastal habitats, including longleaf pine forests, coastal estuaries and salt marshes, maritime forests, and beach and dune habitats. This group presents birders with a variety of opportunities, ranging from short out-and-back hikes to extensive day-trips to the nearby barrier islands. The rare Red-cockaded Woodpecker inhabits the longleaf pine forests of the Croatan National Forest. Wild ponies add to the scenic appeal on many of the islands between Beaufort and Cape Lookout.

Raleigh

You Are Here

© Nate Bacheler

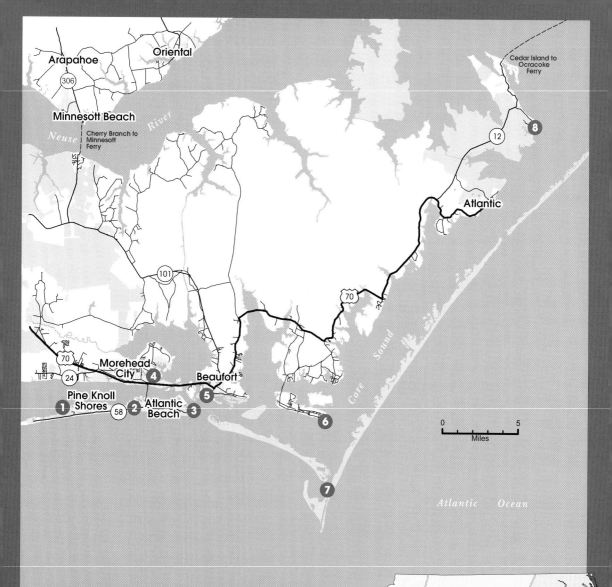

East Carteret Group

1 NC Aquarium at Pine Knoll Shores & T. Roosevelt State Natural Area

2 Hoop Pole Creek Natural Area

3 Fort Macon State Park

4 Calico Creek Boardwalk

5 Rachel Carson National Estuarine Research Reserve

6 Harkers Island Nature Trail

7 Cape Lookout Point, Cape Lookout National Seashore

8 Cedar Island National Wildlife Refuge

NC Aquarium at Pine Knoll Shores & T. Roosevelt State Natural Area

$ ♿ 🚶 📷 🍽 🚻 ❓ 🔭 👥

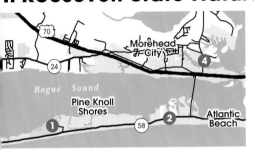

Site Information:
Owner: NC Aquariums, NC State Parks
1 Roosevelt Boulevard,
Pine Knoll Shores, NC 28512
Carteret County
252-247-4003 (Aquarium);
252-726-3775 (State Parks)
www.ncaquariums.com/pks/pksindex.htm

About the Site:

The T. Roosevelt Nature Trail passes through maritime forest and paleo dunes as it winds west roughly 0.75 miles toward Bogue Sound (1.5 miles round trip). This 265-acre maritime forest, owned and maintained by the state, is one of the few remaining expanses of maritime forest on North Carolina's barrier islands. In wooded areas along the trail, look and listen for various warbler, vireo, and thrush species, along with other songbirds. Painted Bunting may be found here during the breeding season. The Alice Hoffman Nature Trail, which leaves from behind the Aquarium building, extends east in the opposite direction.

This 0.5 mile long trail passes along the marsh edge, then enters a forested area. One trail spur extends out to a brackish pond. Scan the marshes for Northern Harrier, Osprey, White Ibis, and Tricolored Heron; listen for rail species.

© Jeff Lewis

Painted Bunting

Species of Interest: White Ibis, Painted Bunting, rails, wading birds

Habitats: maritime forest and shrub, salt marsh

Access & Parking: The T. Roosevelt State Natural Area trail head leaves from the south side of the Aquarium parking lot. This self-guided trail can be accessed daily from 9am to 5pm. The marsh boardwalk, overlook, and Alice Hoffman Trail are only accessed through the Aquarium building, for which there is an entrance fee of $8. The same hours apply. Amenities are available in the Aquarium.

Directions: From the Atlantic Beach Causeway, turn south on NC 58 and travel for 5 miles. At milepost 7, turn right at the signs for the Aquarium onto Pine Knoll Boulevard. Take the second left onto Roosevelt Boulevard. The parking lot is at the end of Roosevelt Boulevard.

Coordinates: N 34°41'57" W 76°49'44"
DeLorme (NC Gazetteer) Page: 78

Rock jetty at T. Roosevelt State Natural Area
© NC State Parks

East Carteret Group

Marsh at Hoop Pole Creek

2

Hoop Pole Creek Natural Area

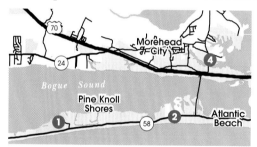

Site Information:
Owner: NC Coastal Federation
NC 58, Atlantic Beach, NC
Carteret County
252-393-8185
www.nccoast.org/education/pubed/naturetrail

About the Site:
This 0.5 mile long trail follows Hoop Pole Creek out to Bogue Sound, passing through maritime forest for much of the walk, and ending with views of coastal salt marsh. The interpretive trail guide gives information about a number of plant species associated with this type of habitat. A variety of migrating and breeding songbirds may be seen and heard in the wooded areas. Look and listen for various warbler, vireo, and thrush species, along with

other songbirds. In winter, Hermit Thrush, Orange-crowned Warbler, Yellow-rumped Warbler, and Ruby-crowned Kinglet are frequent. Scan the creek and marsh areas for Northern Harrier, Osprey, Marsh Wren, wading birds, and listen for rails.

Species of Interest: White Ibis, Marsh Wren, rails, wading birds

Habitats: maritime forest and shrub, salt marsh

Access & Parking: Park at the eastern end of the Atlantic Station Shopping Center, near the Hardee's. An informational kiosk along the nearby forested area marks the start of the Hoop Pole Creek Nature Trail; brochures are available for a self-guided walk. The trail is open daily during daylight hours.

Directions: From the stoplight at the intersection of the Atlantic Beach-Morehead City Causeway and NC 58, turn right on NC 58 and travel west for 0.8 miles. Turn right at the first entrance into the Atlantic Station Shopping Center and park.

Coordinates: N 34°42'04" W 76°45'07"
DeLorme (NC Gazetteer) Page: 78

© Nate Bacheler

Forster's Terns and Bonaparte's Gulls

ort Macon State Park

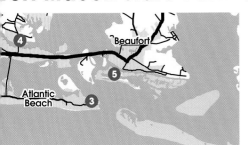

Site Information:
Owner: NC State Parks
Eastern terminus of NC 58,
Atlantic Beach, NC
Carteret County
252-726-3775
www.ncsparks.net

About the Site:

Fort Macon offers opportunities to view a variety of shorebirds, pelagic birds and waterfowl. Winter can be an especially good season to bird here. Walk the beach in a wide arc from the sound side around to the south-facing beach. As the shoreline swings east, it parallels Beaufort Inlet, with views of Shackleford Banks. In winter, watch for loons, Red-breasted Merganser, and waterfowl in the nearshore waters. The occasional Harlequin Duck, Common Eider, or alcid species may be found in the rough surf around the jetty at the southwest corner of the point; look for Purple Sandpiper on the jetty rocks. Scan the horizon for pass-

ing gannets and scoters. Watch for rarities amongst the sandpipers and plovers that frequent the tidal wash areas. In the warmer months, scan for terns and wading birds. Walk over to the Fort and the surrounding forest and shrub areas to look for songbirds, including an occasional Painted Bunting.

Species of Interest: Piping Plover, Purple Sandpiper, Painted Bunting, wintering waterfowl

Habitats: maritime shrub, beach and dune

Access & Parking: Park in the second parking lot, close to the Fort and the eastern-most beach access and jetty. During the summer months, this park can be very crowded; early arrival is recommended. Park hours are 8am to 6pm, November - February; 8am to 7pm, March and October; 8am to 8pm, April, May, September; 6am to 9pm, June - August. Seasonal concessions are available Memorial Day through Labor Day.

Directions: From the Atlantic Beach stoplight at the intersection of NC 58 and the Atlantic Beach-Morehead City Causeway, follow NC 58 east for 2 miles. The road dead ends in the park.

Coordinates: N 34°41'49" W 76°40'40"
DeLorme (NC Gazetteer) Page: 78, 79

4

Calico Creek Boardwalk

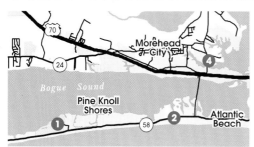

Site Information:
Owner: Town of Morehead City
North 20th Street, Morehead City, NC
Carteret County
252-726-5083

About the Site:

Calico Creek is a pretty nice spot for birding, considering its relatively urban location. The best birding opportunities are at low tide; plan for a two hour lag behind the ocean tide. Walking along the boardwalk, look for migrating shorebirds, wintering waterfowl, and the occasional glimpse of a Clapper Rail amongst the marsh grass. Other opportunities to view the creek are at the ends of 17th, 13th, 11th, and 7th Streets in Morehead City.

Species of Interest: Green-winged Teal, Hooded Merganser, Bufflehead, White Ibis, migrating shorebirds

Habitats: salt marsh, creek

Access & Parking: Limited parking is available along either side of North 20th Street at the boardwalk crossing.

Directions: From US 70 in downtown Morehead City (also called Arendell Street), turn north on 20th Street and go 2.5 blocks to the Calico Creek bridge. The boardwalk runs in both directions along the south side of Calico Creek.

Coordinates: N 34°43'36" W 76°43'45"
DeLorme (NC Gazetteer) Page: 78

© Nate Bachele

Great Egre

Rachel Carson National Estuarine Research Reserve

Black Skimmer

© Harry Sell

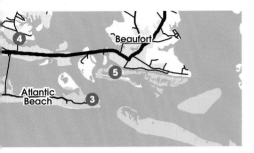

Beaufort

Atlantic Beach

Site Information:
Owner: NC Coastal Reserve
Site is across Taylor's Creek from the Beaufort waterfront; Reserve office is at 135 Duke Marine Lab Road, Beaufort, NC 28516
Carteret County
252-728-2170
www.nccoastalreserve.net

About the Site:
The Rachel Carson site is a complex of islands across Taylor's Creek from the Beaufort waterfront. The islands at the western end of the site – Carrot Island, Town Marsh, Bird Shoal, and Horse Island- are more than three miles long and less than a mile wide, covering 2,025 acres. The site is an important feeding area for both Wilson's and Piping Plovers. A 0.5 mile trail loop, marked with numbered posts, begins at a small beach directly across from the Beaufort waterfront and heads in a clockwise fashion around the western end of Town Marsh. Low tide is the best time to follow the trail. Follow the trail along Taylor's Creek, then head through a salt marsh and a break in the shrub thicket to the top of a sand berm, with views of Beaufort Inlet and Shackleford Banks. Continue on toward mud flats. A wide variety of shorebirds often can be seen probing the mud, including Ruddy Turnstone, Willet, Short-billed Dowitcher and Sanderling. In the fall it is possible to see hundreds of Black Skimmer on the shoal. Head back across the mudflat to pick up the trail again, which continues through shrub thicket, along a tidal creek and eventually returns to the starting point.

Species of Interest: White Ibis, Wilson's Plover, Piping Plover, Black Skimmer

Habitats: maritime forest and shrub, salt marsh, mudflat, beach and dune

Special Concerns: Hunting is allowed within certain areas of the coastal reserve during parts of the year. Birders should be aware of current hunting regulations and seasons and take adequate safety precautions during those times. For more on hunting season safety precautions, see the hunting season information at the beginning of this guide. Footwear should completely cover the foot as shells, especially oyster shells, are very sharp and can cut easily. Marsh communities, like those of Horse Island, are quite vulnerable to the effects of use, and should be avoided. Feral horses also inhabit the islands. Special habitat areas, such as the horses' watering holes and the shorebird nesting sites, are off limits to visitors.

Access & Parking: The Rachel Carson site can only be visited by boat. Visitors may use their own boat or contact local boating concessions on the Beaufort waterfront. Visitors usually land on the sandy beach at the west end of Town Marsh and cross over to Bird Shoals on foot. An interpretive trail guide for the Rachel Carson site is available free of charge over the Internet or by contacting the Reserve education office.

Directions: Enter Beaufort from US 70 and turn right on Turner Street toward the Beaufort waterfront, which is 3 blocks south, along Front Street. Contact one of the local boating concessions to gain passage over to the Rachel Carson site. Or access the site via personal boat from one of many boat ramps in the Beaufort area.

Coordinates: N 34°42'53" W 76°40'04"
DeLorme (NC Gazetteer) Page: 79

East Carteret Group

111

Harkers Island Nature Trail

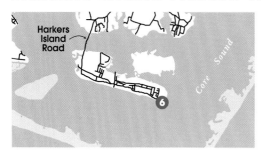

© Walker Golde

White Ib

Site Information:
Owner: National Park Service
131 Charles Street, Harkers Island, NC 28531
Carteret County
252-728-2250
www.nps.gov/calo/

About the Site:

This 0.5 mile nature trail begins directly behind the Cape Lookout Visitor Center. The trail heads north through pine stands and maritime forest, with regular views of salt marsh habitat and nearby Core Sound. Look and listen for Great Crested Flycatcher, Prothonotary Warbler, Painted Bunting, and other songbirds. At dusk, listen for Chuck-will's-widow. Continue on the trail until it becomes a boardwalk, and bear right at a split to reach a spur that extends out into the marsh. Watch for Osprey, White Ibis, other wading birds, and terns. Follow the boardwalk back to the split and head inland to the west. A left-hand turn on the trail will loop back to the original pathway to the south. Straight ahead, the western arm ends just a bit farther along behind the Core Sound Waterfowl Museum (next to the Visitor Center). Retrace your steps back to the Visitor Center. Shell Point, the southernmost point of land near the start of the trail, is a good place to view wintering waterfowl. Watch for Red-breasted Merganser, Horned Grebe, and loons.

Species of Interest: White Ibis, Chuck-will's-widow, Great Crested Flycatcher, terns, wintering waterfowl

Habitats: pine/hardwood forest, maritime forest and shrub, salt marsh

Access & Parking: Park at the Cape Lookout Visitor Center. The visitor center is open daily from 9am to 5pm; the nature trail is open for visitation from 7am to 5pm. The trail begins directly behind the visitor center and ends next to the Core Sound Waterfowl Museum.

Directions: Take US 70 east from Beaufort for 10 miles. Shortly after passing over the North River, turn south on Harkers Island Road and follow this road for about 5 miles south onto the island (Harkers Island road becomes Straits Road). Follow Straits Road, which becomes Island Road (SR 1335) once on Harkers Island, to the east end of the island, where the Cape Lookout Visitor Center is clearly marked.

Coordinates: N 34°41'07" W 76°31'38"
DeLorme (NC Gazetteer) Page: 79

East Carteret Group

Cape Lookout Point, Cape Lookout National Seashore

Site Information:
Owner: National Park Service
Site is offshore on South Core Banks; mainland visitor center located at 131 Charles Street, Harkers Island, NC 28531
Carteret County
252-728-2250
www.nps.gov/calo/

About the Site:

Cape Lookout, located at the south end of Core Banks, is the southern tip of a stretch of undeveloped, natural barrier islands off the central North Carolina coast. A 19th century lighthouse clearly marks the cape. The low-lying point includes extensive dune systems that stretch for 3 miles south of the lighthouse to the south point and then northwest to a dramatic hook. This area is a premier breeding site for the state's beach nesting birds, including Piping Plover, Least Tern, and Black Skimmer. Primary access to Cape Lookout is by passenger ferry. Watch for migrating shorebirds and wading birds while on the ferry, including White Ibis, American Oystercatcher, and the occasional Marbled Godwit or Long-billed Curlew in fall. Upon arrival at the ferry dock, look for migrating songbirds resting in the trees and shrubs. Walk south, either on the sound side or along the beach, to observe a variety of shorebirds, wading birds, and pelagic species. Explore the marsh near the old coast guard dock for rails and other marsh species. The "hook" and the southern tip of the cape

© NC Coastal Federation

The Cape Lookout Lighthouse

host the bulk of the beach breeding birds. Stay out of roped off areas, but be on the lookout for Wilson's and Piping Plovers, Least, Common, and Gull-billed Terns, and the occasional Sooty or Roseate Terns. In early summer, scan the ocean for Northern Gannet and the occasional scoter, storm-petrel, or shearwater.

Species of Interest: Wilson's Plover, Piping Plover, Black Skimmer, Least Tern, Gull-billed Tern, pelagic species

Habitats: maritime forest and shrub, salt marsh, beach and dune

Special Concerns: This area is subject to rapid change due to the effects of wind and waves. Small populations of the threatened sea beach amaranth grow within the National Seashore. Nesting sea turtles and shorebirds are present in the summer. Please respect the posted areas for nesting

(continues)

East Carteret Group

birds and turtles. Hunting is allowed within the National Seashore during certain times of the year. Birders should be aware of current hunting regulations and seasons and take adequate safety precautions during those times. For more on hunting season safety precautions, see the hunting season information at the beginning of this guide.

Access & Parking: Access to Cape Lookout is by ferry or personal boat only. Toll ferries carry pedestrians over from several mainland access points, including Beaufort, Harkers Island, and Davis. Travelers should inquire about up-to-date ferry information at the mainland Cape Lookout Visitor Center on Harkers Island. The Visitor Center is open daily from 9am to 5pm. Note that this site requires extensive walking. Access to and on the island is limited. Soft sand may hinder walking or wheelchairs. There is a wooden walkway from the ferry dock to an observation platform at the beach and to the Keeper's Quarters by the lighthouse. Ease of access to this walkway is dependent on the tide phase. It is a distance of

3 miles to reach the southern most point of the cape and there are no shelters on the island. Restroom facilities are at the lighthouse. Hunting is allowed during certain times of the year. Birders should be aware of current hunting regulations and seasons and take adequate safety precautions during those times. For more on hunting season safety precautions, see the hunting season information at the beginning of this guide.

Directions: Take US 70 east from Beaufort for 10 miles. Shortly after passing over the North River, turn south on Harkers Island Road. Follow this road, which shortly becomes Straits Road, for about 5 miles onto the island. Straits Road becomes Island Road (SR 1335) once on Harkers Island. Follow it to the east end of the island, where the road ends at the Cape Lookout Visitor Center. Ferry operator signs are clearly marked along the road.

Coordinates: N 34°37'22" W 76°31'28" DeLorme (NC Gazetteer) Page: 79

© Jeff Lewis

Red Knot

Cedar Island National Wildlife Refuge

Site Information:
Owner: US Fish and Wildlife Service
NC 12, Cedar Island, NC
Carteret County
252-926-4021
www.fws.gov/cedarisland/

About the Site:

Cedar Island National Wildlife Refuge consists of approximately 11,000 acres of brackish marsh and 3,480 acres of woodland habitat. Sixteen miles of dirt roads and firebreaks provide visual access to the marsh and woodlands, as well as the bays and sound. The firebreaks serve as walking trails. The marsh and estuary provide wintering habitat for thousands of ducks and nesting habitat for colonial waterbirds. Raptors can be seen hunting over the marsh, and songbirds are viewed along the fringe habitats and uplands. On rare occasion, elusive rails may be spotted in the marsh grasses. Travel along NC 12 to bird the extensive marsh system. Listen for Black, Virginia, Yellow, and Clapper Rails, along with Marsh

Wren, Sedge Wren and Seaside Sparrow. Turn down Lola Road to bird in pine woodlands and scrub-shrub thickets. In spring and early summer, this is a good area to encounter migrating songbirds.

Species of Interest: Least Bittern, Black Rail, Brown-headed Nuthatch, Sedge Wren, Seaside Sparrow, wintering waterfowl

Habitats: pine/hardwood forest, moist shrubland, salt marsh, maritime forest and shrub

Special Concerns: Waterfowl hunting is permitted on a 400-acre portion of marsh west of NC 12. Birders should be aware of current hunting regulations and seasons and take adequate safety precautions during those times. Contact the refuge headquarters for additional information and regulations. For more on hunting season safety precautions, see the hunting season information at the beginning of this guide. Prescribed burning is done periodically in the woodlands and marshes. Fire enhances wildlife habitat by promoting new growth and plant diversity, creating open areas, and reducing hazardous fuel accumulations that may result in destructive wildfires.

Access & Parking: The refuge is open daily during daylight hours. However, there are very few formal access areas. Birding is permitted along NC 12; the shoulders are wide enough to safely pull off the road. The refuge office is located on Lola Road; look for signs on NC 12. The gated refuge roads are closed to vehicles, but pedestrian access is permitted.

Directions: From Beaufort, take US 70 east for approximately 30 miles, at which point it becomes NC 12. NC 12 bisects the refuge's extensive salt marshes. Stay on NC 12 for approximately 10 more miles and watch for signs to the refuge office, on Lola Road (SR 1388), on the right.

Coordinates: N 34°57'18" W 76°16'39"
DeLorme (NC Gazetteer) Page: 79

© Walker Golder

Northern Pintail in flight

115

© David Allen

Sunset at Cedar Island

© Jeff Lewis

Common Tern

While You're In the Area

Aurora - Bayview Ferry
Cedar Island - Ocracoke Ferry
NC Department of Transportation,
Ferry Division
800-856-0343
www.ncdot.org/transit/ferry

Core Sound Waterfowl Museum
1785 Island Road
Harkers Island, NC 28531
252-728-1500
www.coresound.com

HomegrownHandmade
Art Roads and Farm Trails of North Carolina
www.homegrownhandmade.com

North Carolina Maritime Museum
315 Front Street
Beaufort, NC 28516-2125
252-728-7317
www.ah.dcr.state.nc.us/sections/maritime/

Welcome to the
Onslow Bight Group

The Onslow Bight Group offers both inland and coastal birding opportunities. Explore a longleaf pine forest in the Croatan National Forest, or visit a maritime forest on the southern end of Bogue Banks. Bring your canoe or kayak if you're up for a paddle trip down the New River, or catch the ferry ride from mainland Hammocks Beach State Park to Bear Island and experience the unspoiled beauty of this barrier island ecosystem.

Raleigh

You Are Here

© Nate Bacheler

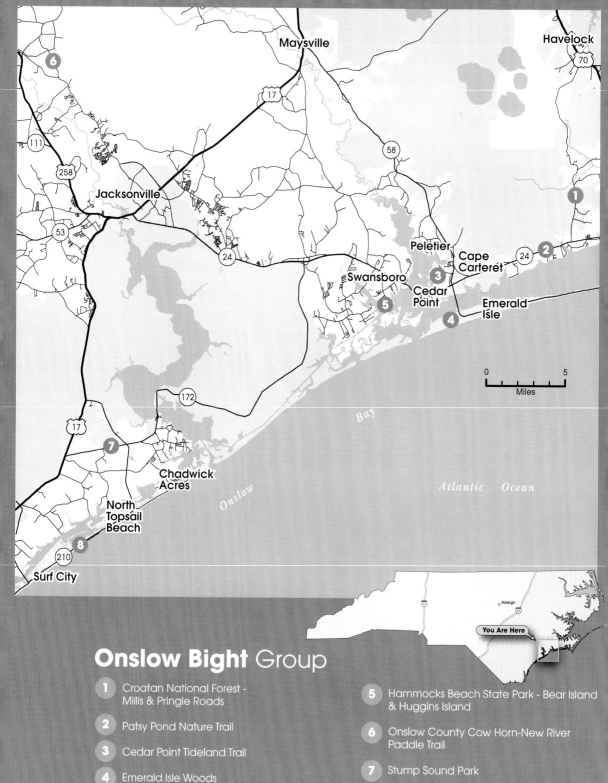

Onslow Bight Group

1 Croatan National Forest -
Millis & Pringle Roads

2 Patsy Pond Nature Trail

3 Cedar Point Tideland Trail

4 Emerald Isle Woods

5 Hammocks Beach State Park - Bear Island
& Huggins Island

6 Onslow County Cow Horn-New River
Paddle Trail

7 Stump Sound Park

8 Onslow County Public Beach Access #2

Worm-eating Warbler

© Harry Sell

Croatan National Forest - Millis & Pringle Roads 🚶 📷 ❓

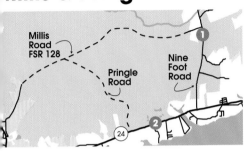

Site Information:
Owner: USDA Forest Service
Millis and Pringle Roads, north of Ocean, NC
Carteret County
252-638-5628
www.cs.unca.edu/nfsnc/recreation/cro-atan.pdf

About the Site:

These two roads present some of the best birding opportunities in the southern portion of the Croatan National Forest. After turning onto Millis Road, look for early successional species, including Blue Grosbeak and Indigo Bunting in nearby fields. Driving this same area at night, listen for owls and nightjars. A gated road on the right (Forest Service Road 3019), approximately 1.3 miles down Millis Road, leads 0.5 miles back to the headwaters of a tributary of the Newport River. Search for Yellow-billed Cuckoo, Northern Parula, Prothonotary Warbler and other breeding songbirds. Soon thereafter begins the Millis Road Savanna, which borders Millis Road on the left and makes this stretch of road especially appealing. Red-cockaded Woodpecker can be found here year round. At 1.4 miles look for a walking trail on the left, which leads past several cavity trees. Also present are Red-headed Woodpecker, Brown-headed Nuthatch, and Bachman's Sparrow. Continuing along Millis Road, stop to listen for Prothonotary, Swainson's, Worm-eating and Hooded Warblers where the road crosses creeks and drains. Just beyond 5 miles on Millis Road, turn left on Pringle Road (Forest Service Road 123). This road passes by

pine flatwoods and offers another opportunity to see Red-cockaded Woodpecker and Bachman's Sparrow.

Species of Interest: Red-cockaded Woodpecker, Brown-headed Nuthatch, Prothonotary Warbler, Worm-eating Warbler, Swainson's Warbler, Bachman's Sparrow

Habitats: longleaf pine savanna, floodplain forest, early successional, moist shrubland

Special Concerns: Hunting is allowed within Croatan National Forest during certain times of the year. Birders should be aware of current hunting regulations and seasons and take adequate safety precautions during those times. For more on hunting season safety precautions, see the hunting season information at the beginning of this guide. Venomous snakes, including pygmy rattlesnakes and timber rattlesnakes, can also be found in the Croatan.

Access & Parking: There is very limited formal parking within this section of the Croatan; take advantage of road shoulders and turn-outs. These roads can usually be driven safely in all types of vehicles, however, sections of road can flood after heavy rainfall. The Croatan National Forest is accessible year round, day and night. Information and maps can be picked up at the Croatan National Forest District Office, located on US 70, approximately 8 miles south of New Bern.

Directions: To reach the start of Millis Road, travel approximately 8 miles west on NC 24 from where it splits from US 70 in Morehead City. Turn right on Nine Foot Road and travel north for approximately 3 miles, turning left on Millis Road (SR 1112), which quickly becomes Forest Service Road 128. Pringle Road, which connects to Millis Road, can be accessed from NC 24, 2.7 miles west of the Nine Foot Road turn.

Coordinates: N 34°46'16" W 76°55'50" (start of Millis Road)
DeLorme (NC Gazetteer) Page: 78

Onslow Bight Group

119

Patsy Pond Nature Trail

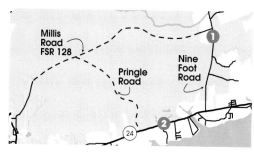

Millis Road FSR 128

Nine Foot Road

Pringle Road

24

Site Information:
Owner: NC Coastal Federation (manager),
USDA Forest Service (property owner)
Directly across from the NC Coastal Federation headquarters, 3609 NC 24,
Ocean, NC 28570
Carteret County
252-393-8185
www.nccoast.org/education/pubed/
naturetrail

About the Site:

The Patsy Pond Nature Trail is part of the Croatan National Forest and winds through an open woodland of longleaf pine forest. Visitors have three trail options, a 0.75 mile trail loop, a 1.5 mile trail loop, or a 2.5 mile trail loop. Red-cockaded Woodpecker can be found here year round. Look for active cavity trees marked with blue bands. Also present are Wild Turkey, Red-headed Woodpecker, Brown-headed Nuthatch, Pine Warbler and other species associated with longleaf pine forest. Signs along the 1.5 mile trail pertain to the self-guided tour brochure.

Species of Interest: Red-cockaded Woodpecker, Brown-headed Nuthatch

Habitats: longleaf pine forest, isolated wetlands, moist shrubland, ponds

Special Concerns: Hunting is allowed within Croatan National Forest during certain times of the year. Birders should be aware of current hunting regulations and seasons and take adequate safety precautions dur-

Patsy Pond Nature Trail

ing those times. For more on hunting season safety precautions, see the hunting season information at the beginning of this guide.

Access & Parking: The parking lot is directly across the road from the NC Coastal Federation headquarters on NC 24. An informational kiosk at the west end of the parking lot marks the start of the trail; brochures are available here for a self-guided walk. The trail is open daily during daylight hours.

Directions: Take NC 24 west from Morehead City for approximately 9 miles. The parking lot is on the north side of the road, directly across from the NC Coastal Federation headquarters. The headquarters are open to visitors 8:30am to 5pm, Monday - Friday.

Coordinates: N 34°43'07" W 76°57'49"
DeLorme (NC Gazetteer) Page: 78

Onslow Bight Group

③

Cedar Point Tideland Trail 〓 ⛺ ♿ 🚶 🏕 🚻 🔭

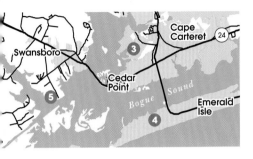

Site Information:
Owner: USDA Forest Service
Forest Service Road 153-A,
Cape Carteret, NC 28584
Carteret County
252-638-5628

About the Site:

This 1 mile long loop trail provides opportunities to view salt marsh and upland pine/hardwood associated bird species. Walk the trail in either direction. A combination of raised boardwalks and paths cross the marsh and pine/hardwood communities as the trail winds around along the edge of the White Oak River estuary. Snags throughout the area offer good

chances to view woodpecker species, including Red-headed Woodpecker. One short dead-end spur provides a nice view of the tidal marsh, with opportunities to view herons, egrets, and Osprey. On rare occasion, Painted Bunting can be spotted at this site. The best birding opportunities here are late April through early June.

Species of Interest: Red-headed Woodpecker, Brown-headed Nuthatch, Summer Tanager, Painted Bunting, wading birds

Habitats: pine/hardwood forest, wetland forest, maritime shrub, salt marsh

Access & Parking: The trail begins at the north side of the parking area and is accessible daily during daylight hours.

Directions: From the intersection of NC 24 and NC 58 in Cape Carteret, take NC 58 north for 0.7 miles. Turn left on VFW Road (SR 1114). Go 0.5 miles and turn left on Forest Service Road 153-A. Travel for approximately 1 mile to the parking lot.

Coordinates: N 34°41'30" W 77°05'11"
DeLorme (NC Gazetteer) Page: 78

Onslow Bight Group

Clapper Rail
© Harry Sell

Common Yellowthroat
© Brady Beck

Emerald Isle Woods

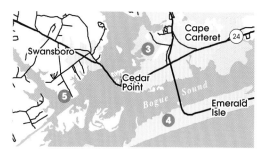

Site Information:
Owner: Town of Emerald Isle
Coast Guard Road, Emerald Isle, NC 28594
Carteret County
252-354-6350
www.emeraldisle-nc.org

About the Site:

Emerald Isle Woods is a 40 acre preserve that provides birding opportunities on the south shore of Bogue Sound. More than 2 miles of trails wind through both pine woodlands and maritime forest. Leaving from the parking area, the trail winds through thickets interspersed with several small wetlands. Look and listen for Wood Duck, Great Crested Flycatcher, Prothonotary Warbler and other songbirds. Heading north towards the sound, the habitat changes to maritime forest. Watch for Red-bel-

lied Woodpecker and Pine Warbler. At dusk, listen for Chuck-will's-widow. A raised wooden boardwalk begins near the restroom facilities at the end of the main road. The boardwalk snakes across ancient dunes and offers views of Bogue Sound and the Intracoastal Waterway. Extending across broad tidal wetlands, the boardwalk leads to a floating dock where kayaks and canoes may be launched. Scan the wetlands and shoreline area for American Oystercatcher, Black Skimmer, terns, shorebirds, wading birds, and wintering waterfowl.

Species of Interest: American Oystercatcher, Black Skimmer, Great Crested Flycatcher, Prothonotary Warbler, wading birds, wintering waterfowl

Habitats: pine/hardwood forest, isolated wetlands, maritime forest and shrub, salt marsh

Special Feature: Emerald Isle Woods contains the highest paleo dune system on Bogue Banks. These ancient dunes were created during the formation and movement of former inlets, emphasizing the ever-changing nature of the barrier island systems.

Access & Parking: Parking is available on site for cars and special group buses. The site is open daily during daylight hours. Canoes and kayaks may be launched from the floating dock, but they must be transported approximately 1000 feet from the nearest vehicle accessible point. Trail maps are available from the information kiosk at the entrance.

Directions: From the intersection of NC 24 and NC 58 in Cape Carteret, travel south on NC 58 over the Intracoastal Waterway bridge. After crossing the bridge, make your first right-hand turn on Coast Guard Road. Travel 0.3 miles on Coast Guard Road to the park entrance on the right.

Coordinates: N 34°39'31" W 77°04'05"
DeLorme (NC Gazetteer) Page: 78

© James Craig

Emerald Isle Woods boardwalk

ammocks Beach 🏖️ 🚤 ⛺ 💲 ♿ 🥾 🏕️ 🍽️ 🚻 ❓ 🔭 🏨

State Park - Bear Island & Huggins Island

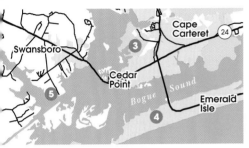

Swansboro

Cedar Point

Bogue Sound

Cape Carteret 24

Emerald Isle

Site Information:
Owner: NC State Parks
1572 Hammocks Beach Road,
Swansboro, NC 28584
Onslow County
910-326-4881
www.ncsparks.net/habe

About the Site:

A venture to Bear Island in Hammocks Beach State Park provides a unique opportunity to explore one of the most unspoiled and uninhabited barrier islands on the coast. Visitors must reach the island by ferry from the mainland visitor center or by private boat. The ride provides great views of marsh habitats, wading birds and shorebirds, especially at low tide. Painted Bunting may be seen near the boat dock on the island and a walk across the island to the ocean side will provide chances to locate

birds in the beach and dune habitats. Once on the ocean side, turn left and walk about 1.5 miles to Bogue Inlet, where both migrating and nesting shorebirds can be seen seasonally. Rent a kayak to explore Huggins Island, which offers excellent opportunities to see shorebirds, wading birds, and maritime forest birds.

Species of Interest: Piping Plover, American Oystercatcher, Black Skimmer, Painted Bunting, wading birds

Habitats: maritime forest and shrub, salt marsh, beach and dune

Special Concern: Nesting sea turtles and shorebirds are present during the summer. Please respect the posted areas for nesting birds and turtles.

© NC State Parks

Access & Parking:
Parking is available at the mainland entrance. Access to Bear Island is by ferry from the visitor center (fee required) or personal boat. The park is open from 8am to 6pm, September - May; 8am to 7pm, June - August. Call the park office or check the web site for the Bear Island ferry schedule. The park has a floating canoe/ kayak launch; the motorboat launch is only available to overnight campers.

Directions: From Swansboro, take NC 24 west to Hammocks Beach Road (SR 1511). Turn south and travel 2.1 miles to the park entrance on the right.

Coordinates: N 34°40'15" W 77°08'35"
DeLorme (NC Gazetteer) Page: 77

© Alan Cradick

Birders on Bear Island

Onslow Bight Group

Onslow County Cow Horn- New River Paddle Trail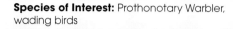

Cow Horn Road

Gum Branch Road

258

Site Information:
Contact: Onslow County Parks and Recreation Department
From Richlands/Steed Park, near Richlands, NC, to New River Waterfront Park, Jacksonville, NC
Onslow County
910-347-5332
www.co.onslow.nc.us/parks

About the Site:

This paddle trail begins near Richlands and meanders down Cow Horn Creek, a cypress lined black water creek, for 3 miles until it empties into the New River. Watch for beaver dams along the first few miles of the trail, and tall limestone cliffs at the confluence of the New River. The trail continues south along the New River for nearly 15 miles to the city of Jacksonville. The river is narrow until the last 0.5 miles of the trail, which crosses open water. Depending on the season, paddlers will have chances to see and hear migrating and breeding species typical of hardwood riverine forests, including Wood Duck, Barred Owl, Prothonotary Warbler, Northern Parula, and a variety of wading birds.

© Brady Beck

Northern Flicker nestling

Species of Interest: Prothonotary Warbler, wading birds

Habitats: floodplain forest, river

Special Concern: Low water may make entry at some sites difficult. Paddlers may encounter fast-moving rapids near dams along Cow Horn Creek and at the New River confluence; downed trees are possible along the river. Abrupt changes in weather conditions can change the difficulty of paddling.

Access & Parking: There are four access points along the trail, all of which are marked with brown paddle-trail signs along nearby roadways: 1) Richlands/Steed Park Landing on Cow Horn Road near Richlands, 2) Henry McCallister Landing, on Rhodestown Road, 3) Onslow County Burton Industrial Park Primitive Landing, off of US 258/NC 24 South, and the trail end at 4) New River Waterfront Park. The third landing can be difficult to drive into after rain events; 4-wheel drive is necessary. Call the Onslow County Parks and Recreation Department to request the Onslow County Cow Horn - New River Paddle Trail map and brochure and to check river conditions.

Directions: To the put-in at Richlands/Steed Park: from the intersection of US 17 and Gum Branch Road in Jacksonville, take Gum Branch Road 10 miles north. Bear right on Cow Horn Road and travel for 1.3 miles to the put-in on the left.

To the take-out at New River Waterfront Park: From US 258 South entering Jacksonville, exit onto US 17 towards Jacksonville. As soon as you pass over the New River/US 17 bridge, turn right on Riverview Street. Drive straight ahead into the entrance of New River Waterfront Park.

Coordinates: N 34° 53' 39" W 77°30'47"
DeLorme (NC Gazetteer) Page: 77

Onslow Bight Group

Stump Sound Park

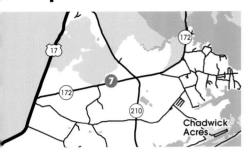

Crested Flycatcher, Brown-headed Nuthatch, Prairie Warbler and Yellow-breasted Chat. Another nature trail, approximately 0.5 miles in length, begins just after the tennis courts, on the right-hand side of the road behind the playground area. This trail is marked with interpretive signs and passes through similar habitat.

Species of Interest: Great Crested Flycatcher, Brown-headed Nuthatch

Habitats: pine/hardwood forest, longleaf pine forest, isolated wetlands

Access & Parking: Daily hours of operation are 10am to 10pm, April - September; 10am to 5pm, October - March. Seasonal concessions available on-site.

Directions: From the intersection of NC 210 and NC 172 in Sneads Ferry, take NC 172 south for 0.8 miles. The park entrance is on the right.

Coordinates: N 34°32′57″ W 77°27′00″ DeLorme (NC Gazetteer) Page: 85

Site Information:

Contact: Onslow County Parks and Recreation Department
1771 NC 172, Sneads Ferry, NC 28460
Onslow County
910-347-5332
www.co.onslow.nc.us/parks

About the Site:

Stump Sound Park is a brief but productive stop to make while birding in Onslow County. A short loop trail, approximately 0.25 miles in length, begins just before the tennis courts on the left. The trail passes through longleaf pine forest with a dense midstory. Watch for Great

© Nate Bacheler

Prairie Warbler

© Walker Golder

Seaside Sparrow

Onslow County Public Beach Access #2

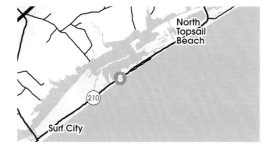

North Topsail Beach

8

210

Surf City

Site Information:
Contact: Onslow County Parks and Recreation Department
2950 Island Drive,
North Topsail Beach, NC 28460
Onslow County
910-347-5332
www.co.onslow.nc.us/parks

About the Site:

This site offers both beach and sound side access. On the sound side, watch for Painted Bunting during the breeding season, in addition to Seaside Sparrow, Eurasian Collared-Dove and White Ibis. The beach side offers opportunities to see migrating shorebirds such as Red Knot and Dunlin. Black-bellied

Plover are also a possibility in all but the summer months. During fall, watch overhead for migrating hawks. In winter, look for Common and Red-throated Loons, Horned Grebe and Northern Gannet just offshore.

Species of Interest: Red-throated Loon, Horned Grebe, White Ibis, Seaside Sparrow, Painted Bunting

Habitats: maritime shrub, salt marsh, beach and dune

Access & Parking: Ample parking is available in lots on both sides of the road. Daily hours of operation are 9am to 8pm, April - September; 9am to 5pm, October - March.

Directions: From the intersection of NC 210 and NC 172, take NC 210 3.5 miles east to the highrise bridge over the Intracoastal Waterway. Continue on NC 210 onto Topsail Island. Once on the island, follow NC 210 south for 4 miles to the beach access, a few hundred yards north of milemarker 12. Signs clearly mark the parking areas.

Coordinates: N 34°27'39" W 77°29'06"
DeLorme (NC Gazetteer) Page: 85

Onslow Bight Group

Croatan National Forest

While You're In the Area

HomegrownHandmade
Art Roads and Farm Trails of North Carolina
www.homegrownhandmade.com

Karen Beasley Sea Turtle Rescue and Rehabilitation Center
822 Carolina Avenue
Topsail Beach, NC 28445
www.seaturtlehospital.org

Sturgeon City Environmental Education Center
4 Court Street
Jacksonville, NC 28540
910-938-5368
www.sturgeoncity.org

Birders on the ferry to Bear Island

Welcome to the
Bay Lakes Group

Most sites within the Bay Lakes Group are centered around a unique natural feature found throughout southeastern North Carolina. Bay lakes, often called Carolina bays, are so named for the bay trees they frequently support. Learn more about Carolina bays, and the theories behind their formation, when you experience these sites for yourself. You can also jump in your canoe and travel down portions of the Lumber River, a beautiful blackwater river, as it flows south toward the state line.

You Are Here

Raleigh

© Nate Bacheler

Bay Lakes Group

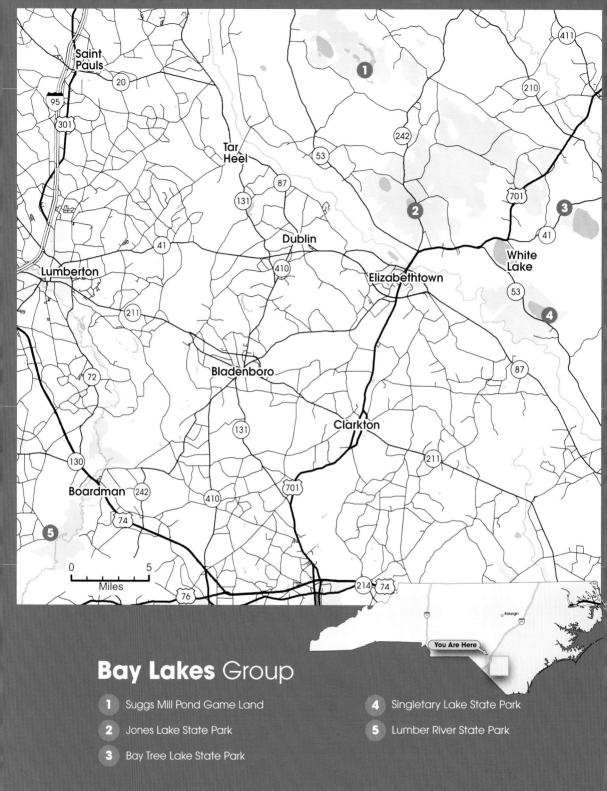

Bay Lakes Group

1 Suggs Mill Pond Game Land

2 Jones Lake State Park

3 Bay Tree Lake State Park

4 Singletary Lake State Park

5 Lumber River State Park

Suggs Mill Pond Game Land

Site Information:
Owner: NC Wildlife Resources Commission
5274 Live Oak Methodist Church Road,
White Oak, NC 28399
Bladen County
910-866-5190
www.ncwildlife.org

Common Nighthawk on nest

About the Site:
Suggs Mill Pond offers good birding opportunities both on land, via the trails and roads
throughout the Game Land, and on Horseshoe Lake, via canoe or kayak. No combustion motors are allowed on the lake. Entering
the property, stop along the road to look and
listen for migrating songbirds. Once at the
boat ramp, walk the road that runs around
the bay lake in either direction. The road
around Horseshoe Lake is approximately 6.75
miles in length, so birders may wish to do an
out-and-back walk. Passing by the managed
waterfowl impoundments along the southern
edge of the lake in the winter, watch for Green-

winged Teal, Ring-necked Duck and Hooded
Merganser. In the spring or breeding season,
watch for Wood Duck, Osprey, Wilson's Snipe,
Anhinga, and wading birds. In the longleaf
pine stands, be on the lookout for Wild Turkey,
Northern Bobwhite, Brown-headed Nuthatch,
Pine Warbler, Bachman's Sparrow and other
pine-associated bird species.

Species of Interest: Hooded Merganser,
Anhinga, Brown-headed Nuthatch, Bachman's Sparrow, wintering waterfowl

Habitats: pine/hardwood forest, longleaf
pine forest, Carolina bay lake, managed
waterfowl impoundments

Special Concern: Hunting is allowed on
Game Lands during certain times of year.
Birders should be aware of current hunting regulations and seasons and take
adequate safety precautions during those
times. For more on hunting season safety
precautions, see the hunting season information at the beginning of this guide.

Access & Parking: From the entrance, follow the gravel road approximately 2 miles
to the boat launch area. The road makes
a right-hand turn at the wildlife depot, approximately 1 mile down the road. Parking
is available at the boat launch area. No
internal combustion motors allowed. It is
highly recommended that visitors request
a current Game Lands Map Book from the
NC Wildlife Resources Commission before
visiting.

Directions: From White Oak, travel approximately 3.5 miles north on Gum Springs Road
(SR 1325). Turn left on Live Oak Methodist
Church Road (SR 1327) and travel for 1 mile.
The entrance to the Game Land is on the
right and is marked with a bright orange
gate and a sign.

Coordinates: N 34°48'26" W 78°39'05"
DeLorme (NC Gazetteer) Page: 74

Bay Lakes Group

© NC State Parks

Sunset on Jones Lake

Jones Lake State Park

Site Information:
Owner: NC State Parks
113 Jones Lake Drive,
Elizabethtown, NC 28337
Bladen County
910-588-4550
www.ncsparks.net

About the Site:

Jones Lake State Park is situated around a Carolina bay and supports birds characteristic of southeastern forests and wetlands. Watch and listen for species characteristic of wooded swamps, including Yellow-throated Vireo, Swainson's Warbler, Yellow-throated Warbler and Prothonotary Warbler. In the wintertime, scan the bay for wintering waterfowl. The rare Red-cockaded Woodpecker also can be seen in the park. Watch overhead for Bald Eagle. Bay Trail is a five-mile loop around Jones Lake, offering an excellent chance to experience the habitats of a Carolina bay. Several short side trails lead to the lake. Begin Bay Trail at the picnic area or campground. The park also has a one-mile nature trail. The Cedar Loop Trail journeys through both the bay forest and sand ridge communities. A canoe ride on the lake provides another excellent way to explore the park.

Species of Interest: Bald Eagle, Red-cockaded Woodpecker, Swainson's Warbler, Prothonotary Warbler, wintering waterfowl

Habitats: longleaf pine forest, moist shrubland, isolated wetlands, Carolina bay lake

Special Concern: The park has an active prescribed burning program; sections of the park may be closed during burns.

Access & Parking: The park is open from 8am to 6pm, November - February; 8am to 7pm, March and October; 8am to 8pm, April, May, and September; 8am to 9pm, June - August. Canoe and paddleboat rentals and seasonal concessions available.

Directions: From Elizabethtown, travel north on NC 242. Two miles north of the NC 53 crossing, look for the park entrance on the left.

Coordinates: N 34°40′54″ W 78°35′44″ DeLorme (NC Gazetteer) Page: 74

Bay Tree Lake State Park

About the Site:

The most prominent feature of Bay Tree Lake State Park is a 609-acre Carolina bay lake. The main access road into the park is a dirt path that leads 0.7 miles from NC 41 to the lake. Once to the lake, visitors can experience a dense bay forest with bald cypress draped with Spanish moss. Bay Tree Lake is shallow; the deepest point is just over 7 feet. Its outline is irregular for a Carolina bay; it appears to merge with neighboring bays. Although its geological values have been degraded by earlier private development activities (note the artificially sandy bottom of the lake and shoreline), the plant communities that flourish here are a haven for many bird species. Along the path toward the lake, watch and listen for species characteristic of wooded swamps, including Yellow-throated Vireo, Swainson's Warbler, Yellow-throated Warbler and Prothonotary Warbler. During winter, scan the bay for wintering waterfowl and watch overhead for Bald Eagle.

Site Information:
Owner: NC State Parks
NC 41, east of Elizabethtown, NC
Bladen County
910-669-2928
www.ncsparks.net

Species of Interest: Bald Eagle, Red-cockaded Woodpecker, Prothonotary Warbler, wintering waterfowl

Habitats: longleaf pine forest, moist shrubland, Carolina bay lake

Access & Parking: Bay Tree Lake State Park is designated as an Undeveloped State Park; it is a satellite park of Singletary Lake State Park. Parking is available in the grass field by the park display on NC 41. The main park road is a sandy dirt path that leads 0.7 miles from the parking area on NC 41 to the lake (foot access only). The park is open during daylight hours.

Directions: From Elizabethtown, take NC 41 east for approximately 12 miles to the parking and access area.

Coordinates: N 34°41'02" W 78°25'45"
DeLorme (NC Gazetteer) Page: 75

Pine understory at Bay Tree Lake State Park

Bay Lakes Group

Singletary Lake State Park ⛺ 🚶 🚻 ❓ 👫

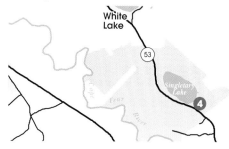

White Lake

53

Singletary Lake

4

Site Information:
Owner: NC State Parks
NC 53 South, southeast of Elizabethtown, NC
Bladen County
910-669-2928
www.ncsparks.net

Species of Interest: Bald Eagle, Red-cockaded Woodpecker, Prothonotary Warbler, wintering waterfowl

Habitats: longleaf pine forest, moist shrubland, isolated wetlands, Carolina bay lake

Access & Parking: Parking is available at the end of the entrance road. The park is open daily, 8am to 5pm.

Directions: From Elizabethtown, take US 701 east for 5 miles. Turn south on NC 53 and follow the signs to the park entrance.

Coordinates: N 34°35'14" W 78°26'51"
DeLorme (NC Gazetteer) Page: 82

About the Site:
Singletary Lake State Park is another of the Carolina bay lakes in Bladen County. The park was developed primarily for organized group camping. The Carolina Bay Loop Trail is an easy one-mile trek that begins near the pier at the lakeshore. Journey through a forest of bay shrubs, cedar, cypress, gum and poplars. The return segment of the trail takes you through a forest of longleaf pine and bay vegetation. The park is home to the Red-cockaded Woodpecker and a Great Blue Heron rookery, along with other birds characteristic of the bay forest. Watch and listen for Blue-headed Vireo, Swainson's Warbler, Yellow-throated Warbler and Prothonotary Warbler. During the winter, scan the lake for waterfowl. Watch overhead for Bald Eagle.

© NC State Parks

Pier at Singletary Lake State Park

Bay Lakes Group

Lumber River State Park

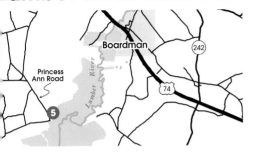

Boardman
242
Princess Ann Road
74
Lumber River
5

Site Information:
Owner: NC State Parks
2819 Princess Ann Road, Orrum, NC 28369
Robeson County
910-628-9844
www.ncsparks.net

About the Site:

Lumber River State Park offers both land and water-based birding opportunities. The Lumber River, the prominent feature of the park, is a designated national wild and scenic river - the only black-water river with this designation in North Carolina. A canoe trip down the river, through typical southeastern floodplain forest, or a quiet walk along the river's edge provides

Lumber River

a unique birding opportunity. Contact the park office for river conditions and suggested canoe trips. Hikers can enjoy the park's nature trail, which is a 1.5 mile loop that begins near the picnic shelter. The trail features a 100-foot boardwalk across a wetland area. A fishing pier and turn-of-the-century millpond are adjacent to the trail. Along the trail, watch and listen for Prothonotary Warbler, Northern Parula, Swainson's Warbler and other birds of the floodplain forest. Be on the lookout for the occasional Anhinga perched in a tree, or Mississippi Kite flying overhead.

Species of Interest: Anhinga, Mississippi Kite, Prothonotary Warbler, Swainson's Warbler

Habitats: floodplain forest, river

Special Concern: Due to the fluctuating water level of the Lumber River, canoeists should exercise caution in planning trips on the river. Add extra time for crossing exposed hazards and sandbars. All float times should include additional time to reach take-out points.

Access & Parking: Parking is available at the Princess Ann Access Area. The park is open from 8am to 6pm, November - February; 8am to 7pm, March and October; 8am to 8pm, April, May, September; 8am to 9pm, June - August. The park office is open 8am to 5pm on weekdays.

Directions: From the intersection of NC 41 and NC 130 near Fairmont, take NC 130 west to Creek Road (SR 2225) for 6.75 miles. Travel south on Creek Road for 3.5 miles to Princess Ann Road (SR 2246). Turn left on Princess Ann Road and the park entrance is two miles on the left.

From I-95, exit onto US 74 east and travel approximately 13 miles. Turn right onto Creek Road (SR 2225) and travel south to Princess Ann Road (SR 2246). Follow directions as above.

Coordinates: N 34°23'21" W 79°00'04"
DeLorme (NC Gazetteer) Page: 81

Bay Lakes Group

135

Sunset on the pier at Singletary Lake State Park

While You're In the Area

Bladen Lakes State Forest
4470 Hwy 242 North
Elizabethtown, NC 28337
910-588-4964

Pond Pine cones

A kayaker's view of the Lumber River

Welcome to the
Pender Group

Pender County offers a rich diversity of habitats, including upland forest, bottomland hardwood swamp and longleaf pine savanna. These places harbor a wide range of birds throughout the year, including numerous sparrows, woodland warblers and woodpeckers. Brown-headed Nuthatch,

Pine Warbler and Red-cockaded Woodpecker are highlights in the longleaf pine savannas, especially at Holly Shelter Game Land. Summer warblers fill the swamps, while sparrows flit among grasses in marsh and dune habitats year-round. Breeding and migrating waterbirds also are common at many sites.

Raleigh

77

95

You Are Here

© Nate Bacheler

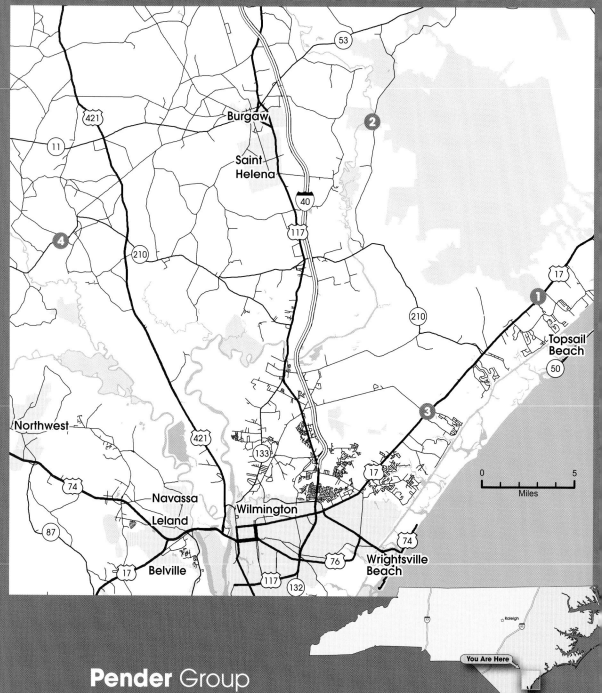

Pender Group

1 Holly Shelter Game Land - Southeast Gate

2 Holly Shelter Game Land - Greentree Impoundment

3 Abbey Nature Preserve

4 Moores Creek National Battlefield

Holly Shelter Game Land Southeast Gate

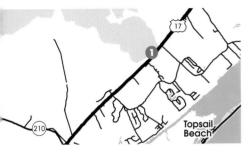

Site Information:
Owner: NC Wildlife Resources Commission
US 17, north of Hampstead, NC
Pender County
910-259-5555
www.ncwildlife.org

About the Site:

Holly Shelter Game Land is one of the birding gems of the state. It contains over 10,000 acres of longleaf pine forest, much of it old growth. The open forest canopy provides habitat for early successional species such as Northern Bobwhite and Bachman's Sparrow. It's one of the best places in the state to see the Red-cockaded Woodpecker. Walk or drive into the Game Land via the dirt road at the entrance gate (Lodge Road). The first few miles of this road offer good opportunities to see and hear some of the classic birds of the longleaf pine forest in North Carolina, especially in the early breeding season. The open pine savanna habitat begins immediately, with patches of turkey oak flanking the road within the first mile or so. Listen and look for Summer Tanager in some of the shrubbier areas. During the breeding season, along the open pine woodland areas, look and listen for Red-cockaded Woodpecker, Eastern Wood-Pewee, Brown-headed Nuthatch, Bachman's Sparrow and Blue Grosbeak. The wetter areas may also yield Swainson's Warbler. In the early morning, or at dusk, listen for Chuck-will's-widow.

Species of Interest:
Chuck-will's-widow, Red-cockaded Woodpecker, Brown-headed Nuthatch, Swainson's Warbler, Summer Tanager, Bachman's Sparrow

Habitats: longleaf pine forest and savanna, isolated wetlands, moist shrubland, early successional

Special Concern: Hunting is allowed on Game Lands during certain times of year. Birders should be aware of current hunting regulations and seasons and take adequate safety precautions during those times. For more on hunting season safety precautions, see the hunting season information at the beginning of this guide. Holly Shelter Game Land is also home to insectivorous plants such as Venus flytraps, pitcherplants and sundews. Do not remove any plant matter - these plants are protected by law.

Access & Parking: Outside of the hunting season, the gate will be locked, but foot travel is allowed. Park just outside the gate, but do not block the gate. When the gate is open you can bird from your vehicle or drive throughout the Game Land and get out to walk, but please be mindful of hunters. This is a three-day-per-week hunting area, so even during hunting seasons, there is no hunting on Tuesdays, Thursdays, Fridays and Sundays (there is hunting on selected holidays). These non-hunting days are best for birding. There are approximately 94 miles of dirt roads on Holly Shelter, and it is easy to get lost. It is highly recommended that visitors request a current Game Lands Map Book from the NC Wildlife Resources Commission before visiting.

Directions: From the town of Hampstead (intersection of NC 210 and US 17) travel 4 miles north on US 17. The Game Land entrance is on the west side of the highway, immediately north of Topsail Baptist Church. Look for a NC Wildlife Resources Commission sign at the gate.

Coordinates: N 34°24'34" W 77°39'26"
DeLorme (NC Gazetteer) Page: 84

© John Ennis

Pender Group

Holly Shelter Game Land - Greentree Impoundment

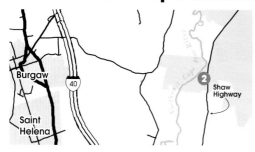

Site Information:
Owner: NC Wildlife Resources Commission
7471 Shaw Highway, Rocky Point, NC 28457
Pender County
910-259-5555
www.ncwildlife.org

About the Site:

This walk will yield birds representative of southeastern floodplain forest habitat. Start by birding around the parking area for Red-headed Woodpecker, Eastern Wood-Pewee, Yellow-throated Warbler, and Summer Tanager. Head toward the orange gate at the southwest corner of the parking lot, which leads to a trail along a dike that runs parallel to the Northeast Cape Fear River. Volunteers of Audubon NC assist with maintenance of this trail, since it was commemorated as the Dave Richie Memorial Trail in April of 2003. This area provides great opportunities to see migrating and breeding songbirds. In winter, watch for waterfowl in the Greentree Impoundment, which is just a couple hundred yards in from the parking area. The trail, which leads to the edge of the Game Land boundary, is just over 1 mile long. Along it, look for Acadian Flycatcher, Yellow-throated Vireo, Northern Parula, Prothonotary Warbler, and Yellow-billed Cuckoo. Near the end of the trail, the habitat becomes shrubby and opens into a pine woodland. Watch for Brown-headed Nuthatch, Yellow-throated Warbler and Pine Warbler in this area. Retrace your steps back to the parking area.

Species of Interest: Red-headed Woodpecker, Brown-headed Nuthatch, Prothonotary Warbler, Summer Tanager

Habitats: pine/hardwood forest, floodplain forest, longleaf pine savanna, managed waterfowl impoundments

Special Concern: Hunting is allowed on Game Lands during certain times of year. Birders should be aware of current hunting regulations and seasons and take adequate safety precautions during those times. For more on hunting season safety precautions, see the hunting season information at the beginning of this guide.

Access & Parking: Parking is available at the boat ramp. Preference is given to those who are trailering a boat and using the ramp. Be sure to park out of the way. It is highly recommended that visitors request a current Game Lands Map Book from the NC Wildlife Resources Commission before visiting.

Directions: From Hampstead, follow NC 210 west for 10 miles. Turn right onto Shaw Highway (SR 1520) and follow it for 7 miles to the NC Wildlife Resources Commission boat ramp on the left.

Coordinates: N 34°32'55" W 77°48'58"
DeLorme (NC Gazetteer) Page: 84

Fox Sparrow

Pender Group

Abbey Nature Preserve

Sidbury Road

17

Site Information:
Owner: Poplar Grove Plantation
10200 US 17 North, Wilmington, NC 28411
Pender County
910-686-9518
www.poplargrove.com

About the Site:

The Historic Poplar Grove Plantation is the oldest peanut plantation in the south with history dating back to 1795. Today, this restored site features period architecture and other cultural attractions set amid a variety of habitats covering over 60 acres, including the Abbey Nature Preserve. Visitors can walk through pine/hardwood forest, a nice patch of upland mature hardwood forest, and an area of open grassy fields. A well-kept 2.5 mile long trail meanders through the site, which includes a millpond that draws Osprey, Belted Kingfisher and wading birds. The trail network allows birders to explore the site in less than two hours, though more time may be needed during spring and fall migration. Watch and listen for woodpeckers, flycatchers and a variety of warbler species.

Species of Interest: Red-headed Woodpecker, Great Crested Flycatcher, Prothonotary Warbler, wading birds

Habitats: pine/hardwood forest, floodplain forest, millpond, early successional

Special Feature: In addition to birding, visitors may participate in any of the many cultural programs offered at Poplar Grove Plantation.

Access & Parking: Park in the Poplar Grove Plantation parking lot. The trail entrance is on the left (north side) of the lot. Daily hours of operation for the Nature Preserve are 9am to 5pm. The preserve is free to visit. The Poplar Grove Plantation house (fee) is open 9am to 5pm, Monday -Saturday; 12pm to 5pm, Sunday. The grounds are closed the last week of December until February 1 each year, and on certain holidays.

Directions: From Wilmington, take US 17 north to Scotts Hill. Poplar Grove Plantation, home of the Abbey Nature Preserve, is on the east side of the highway, opposite Sidbury Road. Watch for building numbers and signs to direct you to the site.

Coordinates: N 34°19'16" W 77°45'56"
DeLorme (NC Gazetteer) Page: 84

Pender Group

© Walker Golder

Yellow-bellied Sapsucker

Moores Creek National Battlefield

Site Information:
Owner: National Park Service
40 Patriots Hall Drive, Currie, NC 28435
Pender County
910-283-5591
www.nps.gov/mocr/

About the Site:

Moores Creek National Battlefield is a unit of the National Park Service and the site of a 1776 victory of Patriot over Loyalist forces in the American Revolutionary War. The park encompasses 88 acres made accessible by nearly a mile of footpaths and raised walkways. Moores Creek itself is a beautiful blackwater stream that meanders through old-growth cypress swamp habitats and draws a great variety of warblers, woodpeckers, vireos and other song-

birds during migration and breeding periods. In addition to the swamp forest, Moores Creek features a long leaf pine restoration area that interprets the history of this unique coastal plain habitat. The close proximity of the restoration area and upland forest to riverine swamp habitats allows birders to cover several habitats in a short period of time.

Species of Interest: Great Crested Flycatcher, Prothonotary Warbler, Hooded Warbler, Summer Tanager

Habitats: pine/hardwood forest, longleaf pine forest, floodplain forest, early successional

Access & Parking: Daily hours of operation are 9am to 5pm. Footpaths and raised boardwalks provide easy access to birding habitats.

Directions: From I-40, take Exit 408 west toward Currie on NC 210. The Battlefield is 1 mile west of the Currie Post Office on NC 210.

Coordinates: N 34°27'27" W 78°06'34"
DeLorme (NC Gazetteer) Page: 83

While You're In the Area

Karen Beasley Sea Turtle Rescue and Rehabilitation Center
822 Carolina Avenue
Topsail Beach, NC 28445
www.seaturtlehospital.org

HomegrownHandmade
Art Roads and Farm Trails of North Carolina
www.homegrownhandmade.com

© Nate Bacheler

Yellow-rumped Warbler

Pender Group

Welcome to the
New Hanover Group

The New Hanover Group offers many coastal habitats to explore, from barrier island inlets to grassy salt marshes. Black Skimmer and Least Tern are easily viewed nesting on several area beaches, while great expanses of tidal salt marsh provide ample opportunity to see wading birds like Tri-colored and Little Blue Heron, and shorebirds such as Clapper Rail, White Ibis, and Willet. In the maritime thickets and forests fringing the marshes, Painted Buntings may be seen and heard during summer. In winter, these same woods become a safe haven for many warblers and sparrows, making this collection of sites a year-round experience.

Raleigh

You Are Here

© Walker Golder

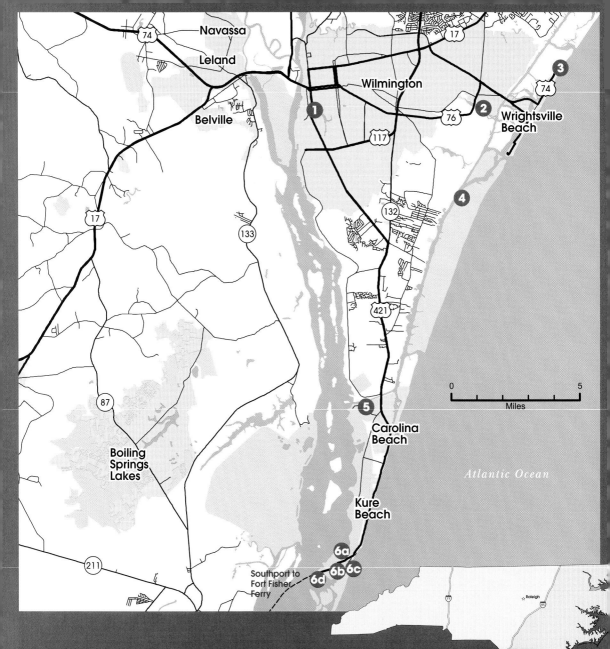

New Hanover Group

1	Greenfield Park	**5**	Carolina Beach State Park
2	Airlie Gardens	**6a**	Fort Fisher State Historic Site
3	Mason Inlet Waterbird Management Area	**6b**	NC Aquarium at Fort Fisher
4	Masonboro Island National Estuarine Research Reserve	**6c**	Fort Fisher State Recreation Area
		6d	Zeke's Island Coastal Reserve

Greenfield Park

Site Information:
Owner: City of Wilmington Parks and Recreation Department
Burnett Boulevard (US 421 South),
Wilmington, NC 28401
New Hanover County
910-341-7852

About the Site:

Greenfield Lake is a historic millpond near downtown Wilmington that has been allowed to return to nature into a naturalized cypress lake encompassing some 250 acres. The lake is ringed by a footpath that affords ample views of open water areas. Waterbirds abound in winter, including cormorants and several species of waterfowl. The walkways and nature trails also allow access to large stands of bald cypress and associated wetland forest plants that harbor breeding warblers, gnatcatchers and woodpeckers. Trees lining the lake's edge provide roosting habitat for herons and egrets that also forage along the lake's shoreline. In addition to the great birding this site offers, Greenfield Lake is renowned for its colorful gardens highlighted by magnolia, azalea, dogwood and moss-draped live oak trees.

Species of Interest: Hooded Merganser, Anhinga, Great Crested Flycatcher, Brown-headed Nuthatch, Prothonotary Warbler

Habitats: pine/hardwood forest, wetland forest, millpond

Special Concerns: American alligators are fairly common on the lake. Feeding them is dangerous and prohibited by law. Wooden foot bridges may be slippery when wet.

Access & Parking: The park is open daily during daylight hours. Canoe and paddle boat rentals, operated by Cape Fear River Watch, are available. Call 910-762-5606 for more information. Other birding opportunities are also available by driving along Lake Shore Drive, which winds around the lake for 5 miles.

Directions: From the intersection of 3rd Street and US 17/76 near downtown Wilmington, follow 3rd Street south for 0.7 mile and turn left at Park Street. Travel about 200 feet and turn left onto Willard Street; the park facilities will be straight ahead.

Coordinates: N 34°12'51" W 77°56'38"
DeLorme (NC Gazetteer) Page: 84

© John Ennis

Greenfield Lake

Airlie Gardens

Airlie Garden

Site Information:
Owner: New Hanover County
300 Airlie Road, Wilmington, NC 28403
New Hanover County
910-798-7700
www.airliegardens.org

About the Site:

Airlie Gardens is a century-old estate turned public garden. It contains hundreds of heritage landscape plants and trees that attract a wide range of songbirds and some raptors. A network of well-maintained paths carries visitors through the gardens and around a series of large ponds that attract a wealth of winter waterfowl, including Hooded Merganser and Green-winged Teal. In addition to breeding birds, such as Orchard Oriole and Northern Parula, the gardens and ponds also attract a great variety of migrating songbirds that use the site for feeding and resting. Wading birds use the ponds for a roosting and foraging habitat. Be sure to stop at the Bradley Creek Overlook and dock for views of terns, shorebirds, and wading birds. During summer, a glimpse of a Painted Bunting might also be possible.

Species of Interest: Hooded Merganser, Brown-headed Nuthatch, Painted Bunting, shorebirds, wading birds, wintering waterfowl

Habitats: pine/hardwood forest, lake, maritime forest and shrub, salt marsh

Special Features: A 461 year-old live oak tree in the gardens is a highlight for visitors. The second Wednesday of every month at 8am there is a guided bird walk through the gardens that is free with the price of admission.

Access & Parking: Hours of operation are 9am to 5pm, Tuesday - Sunday, with extended seasonal hours. There is a $5 entrance fee per adult (children 6-12 are $3). Stop at the visitor center for a map of the gardens.

Directions: From Wilmington or points south: once in Wilmington, take US 76 (Oleander Drive) east toward Wrightsville Beach. Shortly after crossing Bradley Creek, turn right on Airlie Road. From points north of Wilmington take US 17 South and turn left on Military Cutoff Road. Follow Military Cutoff Road for 3 miles. Turn left on Airlie Road and the entrance is less than 0.25 miles on the right.

Coordinates: N 34°12'54" W 77°49'46"
DeLorme (NC Gazetteer) Page: 84

Bradley Creek overlook

New Hanover Group

③ Mason Inlet Waterbird Management Area ♿ 🚶 🚻 ❓

© Walker Golder

Site Information:
Owner: Audubon NC (manager); New Hanover County (owner)
Northern end of Wrightsville Beach Island
New Hanover County
910-686-7527
www.ncaudubon.org

About the Site:

The Mason Inlet Waterbird Management Area is a 300-acre sanctuary located on the north end of Wrightsville Beach. The site is protected year-round for colonial waterbirds and shorebirds to use as nesting habitat during the breeding season, and resting and foraging habitat during winter and migration. Although the Mason Inlet sanctuary is posted with signs and symbolic rope fence to prevent human disturbance to the birds using the area, visitors to the site are afforded excellent views of nesting birds from several vantage points where various terns, Black Skimmer and Wilson's Plover nest close to the fence line. A sandy path beginning at an interpretive kiosk leads visitors across the primary dunes to the beach, following the fence line a little more than half a mile before reaching Mason Inlet. Along the way visitors will see typical barrier island dune and swale plants in their natural setting. During summer, colonial waterbirds and shorebirds nest within the dunes and forage along the inlet shoreline. Ma-

son Inlet mud flats and sandy shoals are also excellent sites to look for migrating shorebirds and wading birds.

Species of Interest: Peregrine Falcon, Wilson's Plover, American Oystercatcher, Least Tern, Black Skimmer, winter waterfowl

Habitats: salt marsh, beach and dune

Special Concerns: Nesting shorebirds and waterbirds are present during the summer. Please respect the posted areas for nesting birds. Sea beach amaranth, an endangered plant, also grows in the dune system. Please avoid disruption of all dune areas.

Access & Parking: Park in the public parking lot (fee) next to the Shell Island Resort or in the next available parking lot to the south. Park only in designated public parking lots. Parking on the roadside, in unauthorized parking at Shell Island Resort, or anywhere outside of designated parking lots will result in a citation and towing. The site is open daily, year-round. Weekly guided beach walks by Audubon NC staff are available free of charge, May - September. Special tours are available by appointment. Contact Audubon NC for scheduling and arrangements.

Directions: From Wilmington, cross the Wrightsville Beach bridge, bear left, and continue to Lumina Avenue. Turn left on Lumina Avenue and follow to the northernmost end of Wrightsville Beach and the Shell Island Resort.

Coordinates: N 34°14'05" W 77°46'34"
DeLorme (NC Gazetteer) Page: 84

WATERBIRD NESTING & FORAGING AREA

© John Ennis

New Hanover Group

147

Saltmarsh Sharp-tailed Sparrow

Masonboro Island National Estuarine Research Reserve

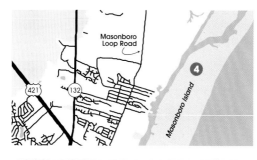

Site Information:
Owner: NC Coastal Reserve
South of Wrightsville Beach Island, north of
Carolina Beach Island
New Hanover County
910-962-2300
www.nccoastalreserve.net

About the Site:

Masonboro Island is a nine mile long undeveloped barrier island located between Wrightsville Beach to the north and Carolina Beach to the south. Masonboro is only accessible by boat and the tidal creeks that meander through the marshes behind this island provide great birding by kayak or small boat. The creeks are inhabited by good numbers of rails, herons and egrets. The dune and swale habitats on the island's backside host sparrows during migration and summer, while the open beach is a favorite foraging area for numerous migrating and resident shorebirds. Because access is limited to boats, the island offers adventurous birding opportunities for those willing to take the extra effort.

Species of Interest: White Ibis, Wilson's Plover, Least Tern, Black Skimmer, Seaside Sparrow, Painted Bunting

Habitats: maritime forest and shrub, salt marsh, beach and dune

Special Concerns: Nesting sea turtles and shorebirds are present during the summer. Please respect the posted areas for nesting birds and turtles. Sea beach amaranth, an endangered plant, also grows in the dune system. Please avoid disruption of any dune plants. Hunting is allowed on the reserve during the fall. Birders should be aware of current hunting regulations and seasons and take adequate safety precautions during those times. For more on hunting season safety precautions, see the hunting season information at the beginning of this guide.

Access & Parking: Masonboro Island is a barrier island only accessible by boat. There are public and private boat ramps in and near the towns of Wrightsville Beach and Carolina Beach. The island is open to public visitation year-round. Kayak rentals are available in Wrightsville Beach.

Directions: Masonboro Island is a barrier island only accessible by boat. The island is south of Wrightsville Beach Island (across Masonboro Inlet), north of Carolina Beach Island (across Carolina Beach inlet) and east of the Intracoastal Waterway.

Coordinates: N 34°09'57" W 77°50'35"
DeLorme (NC Gazetteer) Page: 84

Carolina Beach State Park

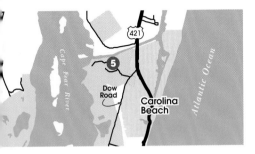

Site Information:
Owner: NC State Parks
1010 State Park Road,
Carolina Beach, NC 28428
New Hanover County
910-458-8206
www.ncsparks.net

About the Site:

Carolina Beach State Park is one of the most biologically diverse parks in the state, with at least 13 different plant communities within the park's 761 acres. More than six miles of well managed trails wind through coastal plain habitats ranging from long leaf pine savanna to riverine shoreline. The open pine forest offers great birding for woodpeckers, grassland sparrows and numerous warblers. The park's wetland forest habitats provide a valuable nesting habitat for songbirds during summer and the park's close proximity to the ocean and Cape Fear River make this site especially attractive to migrating birds seeking shelter and food. During migration, the woods come alive with warblers, orioles, sparrows and the many falcons and hawks that follow them.

Painted Bunting

Species of Interest: American Oystercatcher, Red-headed Woodpecker, Brown-headed Nuthatch, Summer Tanager, Painted Bunting, migrating raptors

Habitats: pine/hardwood forest, longleaf pine forest, wetland forest, isolated wetlands

Special Concerns: Venus flytrap grows in isolated parts of the park, along with other rare plants that are sensitive to foot traffic. Isolated wetlands are home to rare and protected amphibians.

Access & Parking: Park hours are 8am to 6pm, November - February; 8am to 7pm, March and October; 8am to 8pm, April and September; 8am to 10pm, May - August. Park office hours are 8am to 5pm, daily. Concessions are available at the Marina store. Roadside parking is not permitted; park in designated spaces in parking lots.

Directions: From Wilmington, travel south on US 421. Cross Snow's Cut Bridge (Atlantic Intracoastal Waterway) and turn right at the second light on Dow Road. The park entrance is approximately 0.2 miles on the right, on State Park Road.

Coordinates: N 34°02'49" W 77°54'25"
DeLorme (NC Gazetteer) Page: 87

Yellow Warbler

New Hanover Group

149

6a

Fort Fisher State Historic Site ♿ 🚶 🚻 ❓ 👥

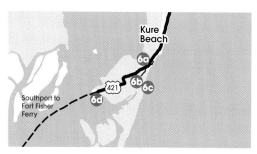

Fort Fisher Battery

© John Ennis

Site Information:
Owner: NC Department of
Cultural Resources
1610 Fort Fisher Boulevard,
Kure Beach, NC 28449
New Hanover County
910-458-5538
www.fortfisher.nchistoricsites.org

About the Site:
The 264 acre Fort Fisher State Historic Site sits between the Cape Fear River and the Atlantic Ocean and contains a mix of maritime habitats that attract numerous birds during spring and fall migrations. Over a mile of trails cover the property, providing access to good birding spots within the maritime forest and on the nearby beach. The evergreen shrub thickets near the southern end of the property offer

good places to look for Painted Bunting in summer, and Loggerhead Shrike and Peregrine Falcon during fall and winter. A grassy field at the southern end of the property contains a low area that fills with rainwater for short periods of time and draws sandpipers and many other kinds of shorebirds.

Species of Interest: Loggerhead Shrike, Painted Bunting, migratory shorebirds

Habitats: maritime forest and shrub, salt marsh, beach and dune

Special Concerns: Visitors must stay on paths because dune plants are vulnerable to foot traffic.

Access & Parking: Hours of operation are April - September: 9am to 5pm, Monday - Saturday, 1pm to 5pm, Sunday; October - March: 10am to 4pm, Tuesday - Saturday, closed Sunday, Monday and most major holidays.

Directions: From Wilmington, travel south on US 421, through the towns of Carolina Beach and Kure Beach. The site is 2 miles south of Kure Beach, on the right. Prominent signs mark the entrance.

Coordinates: N 33°58'18" W 77°55'03"
DeLorme (NC Gazetteer) Page: 87

Sedge Wren

© Harry Sell

New Hanover Group

NC Aquarium at Fort Fisher

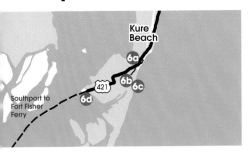

Kure Beach

6a

421 6b 6c

Southport to
Fort Fisher
Ferry

6d

Site Information:
Owner: NC Division of Environment and
Natural Resources
900 Loggerhead Road,
Kure Beach, NC 28449
New Hanover County
910-458-8259
www.ncaquariums.com

About the Site:

The North Carolina Aquarium at Fort Fisher is located adjacent to the Fort Fisher Recreation Area in the southern end of New Hanover County. The aquarium's 24-acre grounds include well maintained trails that are open to the public for free during hours of operation. The trails carry visitors through excellent examples of coastal shrub thicket and maritime forest before opening into salt marsh habitat. Birding for songbirds is best right along the perimeter of the parking lots and in the thickets. The aquarium maintains a large feeding station inside the aquarium gardens which are accessible with admission. Several small ponds on the grounds attract a wealth of migrating birds during the winter months and several types of wading birds year round. The nearby salt marshes also abound with birdlife, including wading birds, sparrows, wrens, swallows and raptors.

Species of Interest: Hooded Merganser, Glossy Ibis, Peregrine Falcon, Indigo Bunting, Painted Bunting

Habitats: isolated wetlands, salt marsh, maritime forest and shrub

Special Concerns: American alligators live in waters in and around the aquarium and while not usually aggressive, visitors should be aware of their presence and not feed or harass them. Parking is limited during times of high visitation (May - August).

Access & Parking: Hours of operation are 9am to 5pm, daily. The grounds can be visited free of charge, but an entrance fee is required to enter the aquarium. Concessions are available in the aquarium. Some activities or amenities are only accessible through the aquarium (e.g., observation platform, interpretive programs).

Directions: From Wilmington, travel south on US 421, through the towns of Carolina Beach and Kure Beach. The aquarium is 2 miles south of Kure Beach. Just past the Fort Fisher State Historic Site, turn left on Loggerhead Road. Go past the Fort Fisher State Recreation Area and travel through the aquarium gates to the parking lot.

Coordinates: N 33°57'46" W 77°55'37"
DeLorme (NC Gazetteer) Page: 87

New Hanover Group

Peregrine Falcon

Fort Fisher State Recreation Area

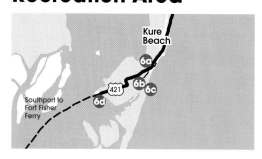

Kure Beach

Southport to
Fort Fisher
Ferry

421

6a
6b 6c
6d

Site Information:
Owner: NC State Parks
1000 Loggerhead Road,
Kure Beach, NC 28449
New Hanover County
910-458-5798
www.ncsparks.net

About the Site:

Fort Fisher State Recreation Area is located between the Atlantic Ocean to the east and the Cape Fear River to the west. Fort Fisher offers miles of unspoiled sandy beaches for birding, swimming and fishing. From the open beach the visitor can venture behind the grass-covered dunes to explore tidal creeks and mudflats where wading birds and flocks of shorebirds forage for food. During the colder months, Fort Fisher is host to migrating and wintering birds that are easily seen from the beach or the access road that runs south behind the beach. The dune and maritime shrub habitats are especially good places to look for sparrows during spring and fall migration periods. During warm months, the salt marshes behind the dunes come to life

Black-bellied
Plover

© John Ennis

with marsh wildflowers and feeding swallows, blackbirds, rails and numerous wading birds.

American Oystercatcher

Species of Interest: Red-throated Loon, Wilson's Plover, Piping Plover, American Oystercatcher, Least Tern, Painted Bunting

Habitats: maritime forest and shrub, salt marsh, beach and dune

Special Concerns: Nesting sea turtles and shorebirds are present during the summer. Please respect the posted areas for nesting birds and turtles. State Park staff are not responsible for towing vehicles stuck on the beach. Removal or disturbance of any plant, animal or mineral is prohibited.

Access & Parking: Park hours are 8am to 6pm, November - February; 8am to 7pm, March and October; 8am to 8pm, April, May and September; 8am to 9pm, June - August. Call the park to check about 4-wheel-drive beach access. Park office hours are 8am to 5pm, daily. Closed Christmas Day. Seasonal concessions are available Memorial Day through Labor Day.

Directions: From Wilmington, travel south on US 421, through the towns of Carolina Beach and Kure Beach. The site is 2 miles south of Kure Beach, just past the Fort Fisher State Historic Site. Turn left into the state recreation area on Loggerhead Road. Parking and the visitor center are on the left.

Coordinates: N 33°57'52" W 77°55'21"
DeLorme (NC Gazetteer) Page: 87

New Hanover Group

Zeke's Island National Estuarine Research Reserve

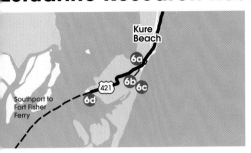

Site Information:
Owner: NC Coastal Reserve
Federal Point, terminus of US 421, south of Kure Beach, NC 28449
New Hanover and Brunswick County
910-962-2300
www.nccoastalreserve.net

About the Site:
The Zeke's Island complex is one of four sites that comprise the NC National Estuarine Research reserve. The 1,165-acre site includes a tidal basin and creeks that draw large numbers of wintering waterfowl that can be seen from the boat access parking area or from the water in a canoe, kayak or small boat. Salt marshes on the mainland side of the basin have some trails that allow visitors to search for sparrows, wrens, wading birds and shorebirds. The dense thickets and maritime forest habitats are also wonderful places to search for migrating and wintering songbirds and raptors. A long line of rocks separate the Cape Fear River. "The Rocks," as this line is called, offer great views of several kinds of shorebirds and the waters on both sides of the rocks host wintering waterfowl. The rocks are difficult to navigate and crossing them is not recommended. Traversing the rocks is not necessary because birding is excellent from the mainland where the rocks begin.

Marbled Godwit

© Harry Sell

Species of Interest: Wilson's Plover, American Oystercatcher, Marbled Godwit, Least Tern, Black Skimmer, Painted Bunting

Habitats: maritime forest and shrub, salt marsh, beach and dune

Special Concerns: Nesting sea turtles and shorebirds are present during the summer. Please respect the posted areas for nesting birds and turtles. Sea beach amaranth, an endangered plant, also grows in the dune system. Please avoid disruption of any dune plants. Hunting is allowed on the reserve during the fall. Birders should be aware of current hunting regulations and seasons and take adequate safety precautions during those times. For more on hunting season safety precautions, see the hunting season information at the beginning of this guide.

Access & Parking: The reserve boundary begins at Federal Point and extends south to include a barrier beach spit, Zeke's Island, North Island, and No Name Island. The NC Wildlife Resources Commission maintains a public boat ramp at the northern boundary of the reserve (Federal Point). The New Hanover County Parks and Recreation Department maintains a pedestrian beach access facility and vehicular dune crossover on Federal Point. The entrance for these is on US 421, just north of the North Carolina Aquarium at Fort Fisher. Access within the reserve is primarily by private boat, though the barrier spit is accessible by foot or off-road vehicle. The reserve is open to public visitation year round. Kayak rentals are available in Carolina Beach.

Directions: From Wilmington, take US 421 south to its terminus beyond the town of Kure Beach, just south of the Fort Fisher State Recreation Area, the Fort Fisher Aquarium, and the Fort Fisher ferry terminal (Federal Point).

Coordinates: N 33°57'33" W 77°56'29"
DeLorme (NC Gazetteer) Page: 87

New Hanover Group

153

Sanderling at sunset

While You're In the Area

Battleship NORTH CAROLINA
Eagles Island
Wilmington, NC 28402-0480
910-251-5797
www.battleshipnc.com

Cape Fear Museum of History and Science
814 Market Street
Wilmington, NC 28401
910-798-4350
www.capefearmuseum.com

Fort Fisher – Southport Ferry
NC Department of Transportation,
Ferry Division
800-368-8969
www.ncdot.org/transit/ferry

Brown Pelican

Halyburton Park
City of Wilmington Parks, Recreation &
Downtown
4099 S. 17th Street
Wilmington, NC 28412
910-794-6001
www.halyburtonpark.com

HomegrownHandmade
Art Roads and Farm Trails of North Carolina
www.homegrownhandmade.com

Welcome to the
Southeast Group

The southeastern corner of North Carolina is rich in natural beauty and offers some wonderful birding opportunities. Along the southern coast, birders have a chance to see species at the northern extent of their range, including the Wood Stork and Painted Bunting. Inland, you can explore Lake Waccamaw, a site rich in endemic aquatic species that are not found anywhere else on Earth. You can also hike in a longleaf pine forest and watch for the Red-cockaded Woodpecker and other species associated with this rare ecosystem.

You Are Here

Raleigh

Southeast Group

© John Ennis

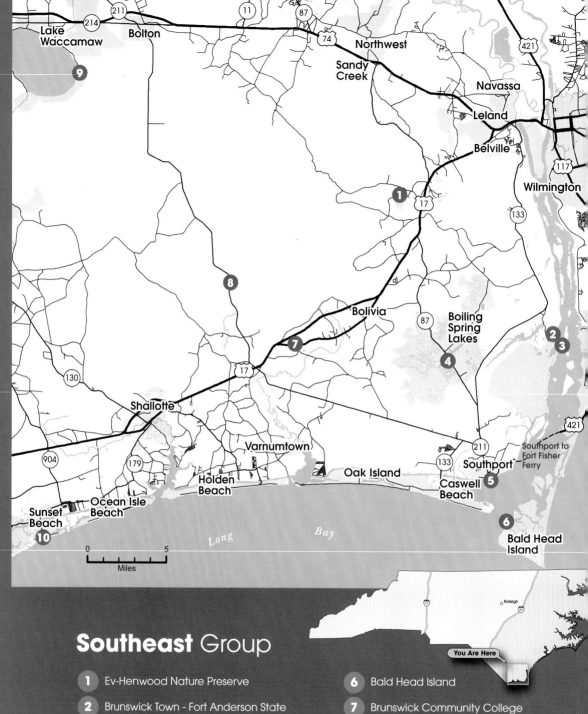

Southeast Group

1. Ev-Henwood Nature Preserve
2. Brunswick Town - Fort Anderson State Historic Site
3. Orton Plantation Gardens
4. Boiling Spring Lakes Preserve
5. Southport Riverwalk
6. Bald Head Island
7. Brunswick Community College
8. Green Swamp Preserve
9. Lake Waccamaw State Park
10. Sunset Beach Island

Ev-Henwood Nature Preserve 🚶 🏕 🚻 ❓

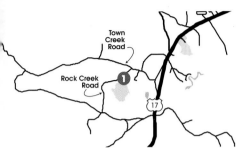

Town Creek Road

Rock Creek Road

1

17

Black Gum and Stewartia Trails for Swainson's Warbler and listen for Barred Owl. Also, walk the trail along Town Creek (the southern boundary of the preserve) to look for waterthrush and other migrating songbirds, plus breeding Northern Parula and Prothonotary Warbler. Indigo Bunting and Blue Grosbeak may be found in the fields surrounding the ponds.

© John Ennis

Barred Owl

Site Information:
Owner: University of North Carolina at Wilmington
6132 Rock Creek Road, Leland, NC 28451
Brunswick County
910-253-6066
www.uncw.edu/arboretum/evhen.html

About the Site:
Ev-Henwood Nature Preserve is a 174-acre preserve in northeastern Brunswick County, donated to UNC Wilmington in perpetuity for the purpose of nature observation and nature education. The preserve presents birders with opportunities to explore both a traditional southeastern floodplain forest and a climax hardwood community. Breeding species and migrants may be heard and located in the vicinity of the two creeks crossed by the entrance road, near the parking area, and on upland trails. Check the floodplain forest on the

Species of Interest: Prothonotary Warbler, Swainson's Warbler, Summer Tanager, Blue Grosbeak, Indigo Bunting

Habitats: pine/hardwood forest, floodplain forest, isolated wetlands, early successional

Access & Parking: The site is open daily during daylight hours. Numerous trails depart from the parking area. Trail maps are available on-site.

Directions: From Wilmington, take US 17 South. At mile marker 39, set trip to zero and turn right on Zion Church Road in 0.6 miles. At 1.3 miles, turn right on Town Creek Road and then left on Rock Creek Road at 2.3 miles. A sign marks the preserve's entrance on Rock Creek Road, at 2.9 miles. Take a left onto the gravel road and follow it to the parking/kiosk area at 3.4 miles. Should the gate not be open, there is parking near the gate, trail maps, and walk-in access to the preserve via the Tulip Tree Trail.

Because Zion Church Road is a loop, if approaching from the south on US 17, set trip to zero at mile marker 37 and turn left on Zion Church Road in 0.2 miles and then left on Town Creek Road at 0.8 miles and proceed to Rock Creek Road as above.

Coordinates: N 34°10'09" W 78°06'56"
DeLorme (NC Gazetteer) Page: 83

© John Ennis

Hermit Thrush

Southeast Group

157

Brunswick Town - Fort Anderson State Historic Site ♿ 🚶 🪑 🚻 ❓ 🧑‍🦽

Site Information:
Owner: NC Department of
Cultural Resources
8884 Phillips Road SE, Winnabow, NC 28479
Brunswick County
910-371-6613
www.ah.dcr.state.nc.us/sections/hs

About the Site:

Brunswick Town - Fort Anderson is a state historic site preserving the remains of a colonial port town and a Civil War era earthen fort on the banks of the Cape Fear River. From the visitor center, walk the trails around Brunswick Pond. This area is reliable for Rusty Blackbird and mixed flocks of songbirds in winter, Prothonotary Warbler, Northern Parula, and Yellow-throated Warbler in summer, and Red-headed Woodpecker all year. Walk along the edge of the Cape Fear River to search for Seaside Sparrow and, in summer, Painted Bunting. Use the wooden stairs at the north end of

Brunswick Town

Battery B and bird the wet areas and tree line near the river. The tree edge from the picnic area to Battery A may produce Painted Bunting, Summer Tanager, and other breeding and migrating songbirds. As you exit Brunswick Town, take a right turn just before the gate. This hard surface road leads to the "Russellborough" House foundation site. Circle the area looking for sparrows and foraging blackbirds in winter, and songbirds during migration.

Rusty Blackbird

Species of Interest: Bald Eagle, Prothonotary Warbler, Nelson's Sharp-tailed Sparrow, Saltmarsh Sharp-tailed Sparrow, Seaside Sparrow, Painted Bunting

Habitats: pine/hardwood forest, wetland forest, salt marsh, maritime forest and shrub

Special Feature: Eastern fox squirrels are also present on-site.

Access & Parking: The trails begin directly behind the visitor center, where site maps are available. Hours of operation are 10am to 4pm, Tuesday - Saturday. The main gate is locked at closing time.

Directions: From Wilmington and points north, turn south on NC 133 from US 17/74/76 at the first Leland exit. Travel NC 133 for 12.5 miles and turn left on Plantation Road. After approximately 2 miles, turn left on Phillips Road, which ends at the entrance to Brunswick Town - Fort Anderson.

Coordinates: N 34°02'24" W 77°56'49"
DeLorme (NC Gazetteer) Page: 87

Southeast Group

Orton Plantation Gardens $ ♿ ⛱ 🚻 🔭 👫‍👦

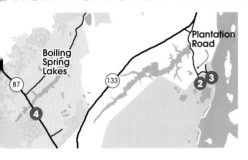

Painted Bunting, and Orchard Oriole. White Ibis frequent the ponds. Watch for the occasional Purple Gallinule or Sora and be on the lookout overhead for Osprey and Anhinga. In the colder months, look for wintering waterfowl on the river.

Site Information:
Owner: David Sprunt
9149 Orton Road SE, Winnabow, NC 28479
Brunswick County
910-371-6851
www.ortongardens.com

About the Site:
Orton Plantation is a historical rice plantation, with a plantation house, colonial cemetery and formal gardens directly on the Cape Fear River. The gardens are best birded during the spring migration and early breeding seasons. Be sure to pay the entry fee before stopping along the entryway causeway. Walk through the various gardens on site, where beginning birders will have good opportunities to look at the birds that reside there. During the breeding season watch for Red-headed and Red-bellied Woodpeckers, Great Crested Flycatcher, Northern Parula, Yellow-throated Warbler, Prothonotary Warbler, Summer Tanager, Blue Grosbeak,

Orton Plantation

Species of Interest: Anhinga, White Ibis, Great Crested Flycatcher, Prothonotary Warbler, Blue Grosbeak, Painted Bunting

Habitats: wetland forest, maritime forest and shrub, salt marsh, river

Special Feature: Be on the lookout for American alligators, another resident species at Orton Plantation.

Access & Parking: There is a $9 admission fee per adult. Hours of operation are 8am to 6pm, March - August; 10am to 5pm, September - November; closed December - February. Concessions are available in the visitor center.

Directions: From Wilmington and points north, turn south on NC 133 from US 17/74/76 at the first Leland exit. Travel NC 133 for 12.5 miles and turn left on Plantation Road. After 0.4 miles, turn left on Orton Road and follow the signs to the entrance.

Coordinates: N 34°02'43" W 77°56'56"
DeLorme (NC Gazetteer) Page: 87

Orton Plantation entrance

Eastern Kingbi

Boiling Spring Lakes Preserve 🚶 ❓

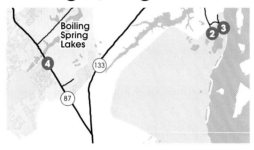

Site Information:
Owner: The Nature Conservancy
Leeds Road, Boiling Spring Lakes, NC 28461
Brunswick County
910-395-5000
www.nature.org/northcarolina

About the Site:

The Boiling Spring Lakes Preserve encompasses half of the incorporated area of the town of Boiling Spring Lakes. The Boiling Spring Lakes Nature Trail allows visitors to walk through a 2 mile portion of the more than 6,000 acres that make up the preserve. Several stops are described in a self-guided trail brochure to highlight the variety of habitats that are present along the trail. The trail passes through dry longleaf pine before entering a pond pine woodland with three bridge crossings over wet areas and ending at another dry pine savanna. As the trail passes through stands of longleaf pine, look for active Red-cockaded Woodpecker cavity trees. Brown-headed Nuthatch, Pine Warbler and other woodpeckers may also be present. In the wetter areas, listen for White-eyed Vireo,

Common Yellowthroat and Summer Tanager. Near the lake, look for waterfowl, grebes and wading birds. Upland shrub areas may present opportunities to see Fox, Savannah, Song and Chipping Sparrow, Indigo Buntings, Blue Grosbeak and Yellow-breasted Chat.

Species of Interest: Red-cockaded Woodpecker, Brown-headed Nuthatch, Summer Tanager, Blue Grosbeak, Indigo Bunting, winter sparrows

Habitats: Longleaf pine savanna, moist shrubland, lake

Special Concern: Venus flytrap, sundew, and pitcher plants are located near and may be observed from the nature trail. Please stay on the designated trail so as not to impact the fragile ecosystems through which it passes.

Access & Parking: The trail begins behind the Community Center. There is a self-guided interpretive trail brochure available at the trail head kiosk. The site is open to visitation daily during daylight hours.

Directions: Enter Boiling Spring Lakes from the south on NC 87. At the light for the high school (Cougar Road) set your odometer to zero. At 1.2 miles, turn left on West South Shore Drive, just before the road crosses Boiling Spring Lake. Make an immediate left on Leeds Road and park at the Community Center. The trail begins at the back of the parking lot.

Coordinates: N 34°01′22″ W 78°03′50″
DeLorme (NC Gazetteer) Page: 87

5

Southport Riverwalk

gazebo, scan the spoil island across the Intra-coastal Waterway for wading birds, Painted Buntings, and raptors. Rarities may include American White Pelican in winter and Swallow-tailed or Mississippi Kite in late spring.

Painted Bunting

Site Information:
Owner: City of Southport
Bay Street, Southport, NC 28461
Brunswick County
910-457-7935

About the Site:

The Southport Riverwalk Trail begins near the city pier and heads west along Bay Street and rounds the small bay of the yacht basin before winding back to a boardwalk on a small peninsula. Wooden signs mark the trail along the way. The pier provides an overlook for the Cape Fear River and Battery Island, which is a prime nesting site for terns and ibis. At the city pier, watch for Sandwich, Least, and Royal Terns in breeding season and Bonaparte's Gull and waterfowl in winter. Proceed west on the trail. At the corner of Bay and Lord Streets, there is boardwalk access to the small beach area. American Oystercatchers and shorebirds may be found here. Continue west around the yacht basin, watching for herons and other wading birds. At the trail's end, walk out on the boardwalk through the salt marsh to the gazebo. You may find Clapper Rail, Seaside Sparrow, and Painted Bunting in the marsh and the cedars and bushes that line the board-walk. At the

Species of Interest: White Ibis, Glossy Ibis, Seaside Sparrow, Painted Bunting, raptors, terns

Habitats: salt marsh, maritime forest and shrub, beach

Access & Parking: Parking is available at Waterfront Park and along Bay Street. Maps of the Riverwalk Trail may be picked up at the Visitor Center, at 113 West Moore Street. The Visitor Center is open from 10am to 5pm, Monday - Saturday. The Riverwalk may be accessed any time of day. Strictly honor "No Parking" signs, especially near the Southport Marina, and do not use private piers.

Directions: If arriving from NC 211 South (Southport-Supply Road SE), Waterfront Park is 1.5 miles beyond the intersection of NC 211 (Howe Street) and NC 87. When NC 211 turns to the left in downtown Southport, stay straight toward the water. The parking lot for Waterfront Park is directly ahead, at the intersection of Howe and Bay Streets. The guided portion of the trail begins just west of the parking lot.

If arriving by the NC Ferry, enter Southport from NC 211, which becomes East Moore Street. Turn left on Howe Street, which ends at Bay Street. The parking lot at Waterfront Park is across from the intersection of Howe and Bay Streets.

Coordinates: N 33°55'02" W 78°01'04"
DeLorme (NC Gazetteer) Page: 87

© John Ennis

Southeast Group

161

Bald Head Island

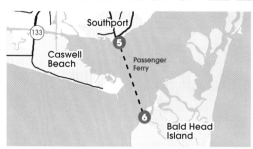

Great Egre

oak trees near the Old Baldy Lighthouse are typically warbler hot-spots during migration. A variety of raptors can be seen in fall and winter

Site Information:
Owner: Bald Head Island Conservancy
Conservancy Office: 7000 Federal Road,
Bald Head Island, NC 28461
Brunswick County
910-457-0089
www.bhic.org

About the Site:

A little over 3 miles long and less than 1 mile wide in most areas, Bald Head Island boasts 14 miles of pristine beach, including Cape Fear Point, the southernmost cape in North Carolina. There are 10,000 acres of salt marsh and approximately 180 acres of protected maritime forest. A variety of shorebirds are visible year-round. Depending on the season you can expect to see American Oystercatcher, Royal, Least, Sandwich, Caspian and Common Tern, Wilson's Plover, Piping Plover, Black-bellied Plover, Red Knot, Dunlin, Short-billed Dowitcher, Whimbrel, Willet and Sanderling. Gannets and scoters are commonly seen flying by the Point from late fall through early spring. A walk up East Beach can be rewarding, especially during migration, as large flocks of shorebirds are present and development becomes non-existent after a short distance. A walk along the Kent Mitchell Nature Trail and nearby Federal Road are great spots to see Painted Bunting, especially from May-July. The golf course lagoons provide opportunities every season. Wintering duck species include the Ring-necked Duck, Hooded Merganser, Bufflehead, Ruddy Duck, and Blue and Green-winged Teal; Glossy Ibis are an uncommon visitor to the lagoons every spring. The large

Species of Interest: Wilson's Plover, Piping Plover, Sandwich Tern, Least Tern, Painted Bunting, wintering waterfowl

Habitats: salt marsh, maritime forest and shrub, beach and dune, golf course lagoons

Special Features & Concerns: The Bald Head Island Conservancy offers year-round environmental education programs; guided birding tours may also be arranged with advanced notice. Nesting sea turtles and shorebirds are present in the summer time. Please respect the posted areas for nesting birds and turtles. Sea beach amaranth, an endangered plant, also grows in the dunes on the island. Please avoid disruption of any dune plants.

Access & Parking: Access to the island is via passenger ferry ($15 fee) from Southport, NC. The first ferry departs the mainland at 6am; the last ferry off-island is at 10:30pm. Once on the island, the best way to get around is either by renting a golf cart or a bike from a local vendor.

Directions: Bald Head Island is accessed via passenger ferry from Indigo Plantation in Southport, NC. Coming into Southport on NC 211 (Howe Street), turn right on West 9th Street. Follow West 9th Street into Indigo Plantation to the ferry landing and parking lots.

Coordinates: N 33°52'35" W 78°00'04"
DeLorme (NC Gazetteer) Page: 87

Southeast Group

7

Brunswick Community College ♿ 🚶 🌳 🏢 ❓ 🔭

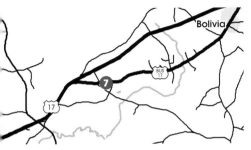

and Prothonotary Warbler, various woodpeckers and wintering waterfowl may also be seen around the beaver pond. Take the upland trail from the blind to the wetlands at the trail's end and watch for migrating and nesting warblers and other songbirds. The site map provides locations for butterfly, victory, and other gardens plus picnic areas.

Site Information:
Owner: NC Community Colleges
50 College Road (NE), Bolivia, NC 28422
Brunswick County
910-755-7300 or 800-754-1050
www.brunswickcc.edu/birdtrailmap.pdf

About the Site:
As you drive onto the campus, watch for waterfowl, wading birds and shorebirds around the aquaculture ponds. The ponds and dense shrubland area behind them may be accessible during normal business hours. Watch for birds along the tree edge by the trail to the eagle blind and scan the beaver pond from behind the blind. In addition to Bald Eagle, Anhinga,

Species of Interest: Bald Eagle, Anhinga, Red-headed Woodpecker, Great Crested Flycatcher, Brown-headed Nuthatch, Prothonotary Warbler

Habitats: pine/hardwood forest, longleaf pine forest, small wetland communities

Special Features & Concerns: Nesting Bald Eagles occur on site. Birders must use the viewing blind and respect posted signs to minimize disturbance of the birds. Eastern fox squirrels are also present onsite.

Access & Parking: The College is accessible daily, during daylight hours. A site brochure with directions, parking information, a map, and a bird list is available at a small kiosk on the left front of Building H.

Directions: From Wilmington, take US 17 South. The entrance to the College is on the left 0.3 miles south of mile marker 25. Proceed past the aquaculture ponds on the right to the Aquaculture Building (Building H), the first building on the right. Parking information is available at the kiosk in front of Building H.

Coordinates: N 34°02'17" W 78°13'47"
DeLorme (NC Gazetteer) Page: 87

Bald Eagle

8

Green Swamp Preserve

© Harry Sell

Bachman's Sparrow

Site Information:
Owner: The Nature Conservancy
NC 211, 5.7 miles north of Supply, NC
Brunswick County
910-395-5000
www.nature.org/northcarolina

About the Site:

The Green Swamp contains some of the country's finest examples of longleaf pine savannas. Much of the preserve, however, is dense, evergreen shrubland. A one mile long trail provides the only formal access into the preserve. This trail leaves from the parking area next to the borrow pit and bears right just beyond the pond, passing through a pine plantation until it reaches a wet area where a short boardwalk (which may be difficult to find in the dense shrub) begins. The trail continues across two more drains and three savannas before tapering off to nothing. The first savanna, Shoestring Savanna, is the best area for birding. Look for active Red-cockaded Woodpecker cavity trees and listen for Northern Bobwhite, Pine Warbler, and Bachman's Sparrow, among others. In the wetter areas during the breeding season, Worm-eating, Swainson's, Prothonotary, Hooded and Prairie Warblers may also be present. Access to the preserve is otherwise limited due to the fragile ecosystems present.

Species of Interest: Chuck-will's-widow, Red-cockaded Woodpecker, Brown-headed Nuthatch, Swainson's Warbler, Bachman's Sparrow

Habitats: longleaf pine savanna and forest, moist shrubland

Special Concerns: Hunting is allowed on the preserve during certain times of year. Birders should be aware of current hunting regulations and seasons and take adequate safety precautions during those times. For more on hunting season safety precautions, see the hunting season information at the beginning of this guide. Venomous snakes are present on-site. Please note that the trails into the Green Swamp are very primitive. At times, the trails in the longleaf pine savannas have been overrun with foot traffic, damaging the fragile ecosystem. Please minimize disturbance along the trails.

Access & Parking: Park in the designated parking area on the east side of NC 211, next to a borrow-pit pond. The site is open to visitation daily during daylight hours.

Directions: From the intersection of NC 211 and US 17 in Supply, take NC 211 5.7 miles north to reach the Green Swamp Preserve. A small green sign designates the parking area on the right.

Coordinates: N 34°05'34" W 78°17'57"
DeLorme (NC Gazetteer) Page: 86

Southeast Group

9

Lake Waccamaw State Park

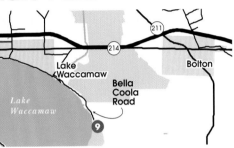

© NC State Parks

Site Information:
Owner: NC State Parks
1866 State Park Road,
Lake Waccamaw, NC 28450
Columbus County
910-646-4748
www.ncsparks.net

About the Site:
Lake Waccamaw State Park is home to the largest Carolina Bay lake in the state and houses a diversity of unique plant and animal species. The best way to experience the park is by walking the Lake Trail, which extends for 5 miles along Lake Waccamaw's natural shoreline from the park's visitor center to the lake dam, where the Waccamaw River begins. Boardwalks, sun shelters and a pier are accessible from this trail. Watch and listen along the trail for Brown-headed Nuthatch, Northern Parula, Prothonotary Warbler, White-eyed Vireo, and other breeding and migrating species. During the winter, waterfowl can be seen on the lake, along with Osprey and the occasional Bald Eagle. Other trails in the park include the Pine Woods Trail (2.5 miles in length), and the Loblolly Trail (a 1 mile loop), both of which depart near the visitor center, and the Sand Ridge Nature Trail (0.75 mile loop), which begins near the day-use area beyond the visitor center. Bring a canoe and explore the shallow lake from the water side. There is no boat access in the park, but two free public boat launch areas are available nearby.

Species of Interest: Bald Eagle, Brown-headed Nuthatch, Prothonotary Warbler, wintering waterfowl

Habitats: longleaf pine forest, isolated wetlands, Carolina bay, moist shrubland

Special Feature: All Carolina bays are unusual, yet Lake Waccamaw is probably the most unique. While many bays are small, averaging about 500 feet in length, Lake Waccamaw covers nearly 9,000 acres and has 14 miles of shoreline. Many bays are also totally dependent on rainfall, but Lake Waccamaw gets its water supply from the Friar Swamp drainage. Most Carolina bays also have naturally high levels of acid, making the water unable to sustain a large diversity of aquatic life. Limestone bluffs along Lake Waccamaw's north shore neutralize the lake's water, making make it suitable for many species of plants and animals. Several fish, freshwater mussel, and snail species are endemic to the lake, meaning they are not found anywhere else on Earth.

Access & Parking: Parking is available at the visitor center lot or at the day-use area, located 1.8 miles south of the visitor center on State Park Drive. The park is open from 8am to 6pm, November - February; 8am to 7pm, March and October; 8am to 8pm, April, May, and September; 8am to 9pm, June - August.

Directions: From the town of Lake Waccamaw, travel east on NC 214 (Sam Potts Highway) to the intersection of Jefferson Road. Turn right on Jefferson Road and travel south toward the lake. Turn left on Bella Coola Road (SR 1947) and the park entrance will be approximately 3 miles on the left.

Coordinates: N 34°16'41" W 78°27'56"
DeLorme (NC Gazetteer) Page: 82

Southeast Group

10

Sunset Beach Island ♿ 🚻

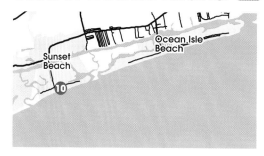

Wood Storks on the marsh

Site Information:
Owner: Town of Sunset Beach
Island of Sunset Beach, NC
Brunswick County
910-579-3808

About the Site:

After crossing onto the causeway, stop just beyond the boat launch on the right to watch for Wood Stork from late spring to mid-fall, and Seaside, Nelson's and Saltmarsh Sharp-tailed Sparrows in the marsh grass in fall and winter. On the flats, watch for shorebirds, wading birds and American Oystercatcher. The causeway ends at a T-junction. In the winter, go straight ahead into the town's free parking lot and walk to the beach to look for scoters, loons, Horned Grebe, Northern Gannet and other wintering waterfowl. Explore the east end of Sunset Beach by turning east on Main Street from the T-junction. Main Street forms a "U" with Canal Drive. Return on Canal Drive for 0.5 miles, then turn right on Cobia Street and then right on North Shore Drive East. Listen and watch for Painted Bunting and Loggerhead Shrike in the shrubby open areas. Parking in right-of-ways along the street will afford views of the surrounding saltmarsh. A spotting scope is useful. Returning to Main Street, head to the west end of the island, where a small parking lot on the right affords views of the saltmarsh

directly ahead. Scan for wading birds and rails. Use the beach access to cross the dunes and explore west toward Bird Island, scanning for Wilson's Plover and Least Tern.

Species of Interest: Horned Grebe, Wood Stork, American Oystercatcher, Black Skimmer, Painted Bunting, winter sparrows

Habitats: salt marsh, maritime shrub, beach and dune

Special Feature: Do not climb on any sand dunes. Observe roadside parking designations closely.

Access & Parking: Public parking is available in the lot at the T-junction, and as designated on streets throughout the island. Roadside parking is also available in many places. During the high season, the traffic waiting at the single-land swing bridge can be quite heavy in both directions; take advantage of early-morning arrival. Public restrooms are available at the public beach access at the T-junction of Sunset Boulevard and Main Street.

Directions: From the intersection of US 17 and NC 904, go east on NC 904. Travel for 3.5 miles to the second stoplight. Turn right on Sunset Boulevard. At 5.3 miles, stay straight where NC 179 Business turns right. There is a light before a single lane bridge that leads onto the island of Sunset Beach. After passing along a causeway, Sunset Boulevard ends at a T-junction with Main Street on the island.

Coordinates: N 33°52'06" W 78°30'25"
DeLorme (NC Gazetteer) Page: 86

Southeast Group

Canoers on Lake Waccamaw

Ruddy Turnstones

Boiling Spring Lakes Nature Trail

While You're In the Area

HomegrownHandmade
Art Roads and Farm Trails of North Carolina
www.homegrownhandmade.com

North Carolina Maritime Museum at Southport
116 North Howe Street
Southport, NC 28461
910-457-0003
www.ah.dcr.state.nc.us/sections/maritime/branches/southport_default.htm

Southport – Fort Fisher Ferry
NC Department of Transportation,
Ferry Division
800-368-8969
www.ncdot.org/transit/ferry

Red-headed Woodpecker

Group		Site Number and Name	Birders Guide to Coastal NC[1]	Birding NC[2]	NC Wildlife Viewing Guide[3]	Hunting	Paddle Trail	Boat Access	Fee
Northeast	1	Dismal Swamp State Natural Area							
	2	Dismal Swamp Canal Trail							
	3	Regional Fitness Trail							
	4	North River Game Land - Harrison Tract				•			
	5	Mackay Island National Wildlife Refuge	•		•	•			
	6a	Outer Banks Center for Wildlife Education							
	6b	Currituck Banks National Estuarine Research Reserve	•		•	•			
	6c	Currituck National Wildlife Refuge	•		•	•			
Tri-County	1	Edenton National Fish Hatchery				•			
	2	Bennett's Millpond							
	3	Catherine Creek/Warwick Creek Paddle Trail					•	•	
	4	Merchants Millpond State Park							
	5	Mill Creek Paddle Trail					•	•	
	6	Upper Perquimans River Trail						•	
I-95 Corridor	1	Roanoke Canal Museum & Trail							
	2	Roanoke River Paddle Trail- Weldon	•		•	•	•		
	3	Northampton County Nature Trail							
	4	Tar River Trail							
Roanoke	1	Morningstar Nature Refuge							
	2	Roanoke River Paddle Trail- Mainstem	•	•	•	•	•	•	
	3	Roanoke River National Wildlife Refuge	•		•	•			
	4	Roanoke River Paddle Trail-Cashie River	•			•	•		
	5	Cashie Wetlands Walk							
	6	Historic Hope Plantation							•
	7	Rail Switch Nature Trail							
	8	Roanoke River Paddle Trail- Conaby Creek					•	•	•
	9	Van Swamp Game Land				•			
Albemarle Peninsula	1	Pocosin Lakes National Wildlife Refuge	•		•	•			
	2	Pettigrew State Park	•		•	•			
	3	Eastern 4-H Environmental Education Conference Center							
	4	Scuppernong River Boardwalk							
	5	Palmetto-Peartree Preserve		•[4]		•			
	6	Alligator River National Wildlife Refuge	•	•	•	•			
	7	Gull Rock Game Land - Outfall Canal Tract	•		•	•			
	8	Mattamuskeet National Wildlife Refuge	•	•	•	•			
	9	Swanquarter National Wildlife Refuge	•		•	•			
Outer Banks	1	The Elizabethan Gardens	•	•[4]					•
	2	Roanoke Island Marsh Game Land	•			•			

Group		Site Number and Name	Birders Guide to Coastal NC[1]	Birding NC[2]	NC Wildlife Viewing Guide[3]	Hunting	Paddle Trail	Boat Access	Fee
Outer Banks	3	Jockey's Ridge State Park	•	•[4]	•				
	4	Cape Hatteras National Seashore - Bodie Island	•		•	•			
	5	Pea Island National Wildlife Refuge	•	•	•				
Southern Outer Banks	1	Cape Hatteras National Seashore - Hatteras Island	•	•	•	•			
	2	Seabirding Pelagic Trips	•	•				•	•
	3	Cape Hatteras National Seashore - Ocracoke Island	•	•	•	•			
Central Coastal Plain	1	CSS Neuse State Historic Site							
	2	Contentnea Creek Paddle Trail					•	•	
	3	River Park North			•				
	4	Stewart Parkway River Walk							
	5	Goose Creek State Park	•		•				
Western Coastal Plain	1	Howell Woods Environmental Learning Center			•		•		
	2	Cliffs of the Neuse State Park			•				
	3	Cabin Lake County Park							•
	4	Jackson Farm							
Lower Neuse	1	Weyerhaeuser's Cool Springs Environmental Education Center		•[4]		•			
	2	Croatan National Forest - Island Creek	•			•			
	3	Croatan National Forest - Neusiok Trail	•			•			
	4	Cherry Branch - Minnesott Ferry	•					•	
	5	Goose Creek Game Land - Spring Creek Impoundment	•		•	•			
East Carteret	1	NC Aquarium at Pine Knoll Shores & T. Roosevelt State Natural Area	•		•				•
	2	Hoop Pole Creek Natural Area	•						
	3	Fort Macon State Park	•		•				
	4	Calico Creek Boardwalk	•						
	5	Rachel Carson National Estuarine Research Reserve	•						
	6	Harkers Island Nature Trail	•						
	7	Cape Lookout Point	•		•	•		•	•
	8	Cedar Island National Wildlife Refuge	•		•	•			
Onslow Bight	1	Croatan National Forest - Millis and Pringle Roads	•	•	•	•			
	2	Patsy Pond Nature Trail		•	•	•			
	3	Cedar Point Tideland Trail							
	4	Emerald Isle Woods							
	5	Hammocks Beach State Park	•		•			•	

Site Index

Group		Site Number and Name	Birders Guide to Coastal NC[1]	Birding NC[2]	NC Wildlife Viewing Guide[3]	Hunting	Paddle Trail	Boat Access	Fee
Onslow Bight	6	Onslow County Cow Horn-New River Paddle Trail					•		
	7	Stump Sound Park							
	8	Onslow County Public Beach Access #2	•						
Bay Lakes	1	Suggs Mill Pond Game Land				•			
	2	Jones Lake State Park			•				
	3	Bay Tree Lake State Park							
	4	Singletary Lake State Park							
	5	Lumber River State Park			•				
Pender	1	Holly Shelter Game Land - Southeast Gate	•		•	•			
	2	Holly Shelter Game Land - Greentree Impoundment	•		•	•			
	3	Abbey Nature Preserve							•
	4	Moores Creek National Battlefield							
New Hanover	1	Greenfield Park	•	•[4]					
	2	Airlie Gardens	•						•
	3	Mason Inlet Waterbird Management Area	•						
	4	Masonboro Island	•		•	•	•	•	
	5	Carolina Beach State Park	•						
	6a	Fort Fisher State Historic Site	•						
	6b	NC Aquarium at Fort Fisher	•						•
	6c	Fort Fisher State Recreation Area	•	•	•				
	6d	Zeke's Island Coastal Reserve	•			•			
Southeast	1	Ev-Henwood Nature Preserve							
	2	Brunswick Town - Fort Anderson State Historic Site	•						
	3	Orton Plantation Gardens	•						•
	4	Boiling Spring Lakes Preserve							
	5	Southport Riverwalk	•						
	6	Bald Head Island	•		•			•	•
	7	Brunswick Community College							
	8	Green Swamp Preserve	•	•		•			
	9	Lake Waccamaw State Park		•	•				
	10	Sunset Beach Island	•	•					

Footnotes:

1 Site listed in *A Birders Guide to Coastal North Carolina*, by John O. Fussell III
2 Site listed in *Birding North Carolina*, edited by Mark Johns and Marshall Brooks
3 Site listed in the *North Carolina Wildlife Viewing Guide*, by Charles E. Roe
4 On-line information only, go to www.carolinabirdclub.org

North Carolina
Birding Trail
mountains • piedmont • coast

NC Birding Trail
NC Wildlife Resources Commission
1722 Mail Service Center
Raleigh, NC 27699-1722
(919) 604-5183
www.ncbirdingtrail.org

info@ncbirdingtrail.org

*I stopped by because of the
North Carolina Birding Trail.*

North Carolina
Birding Trail
mountains • piedmont • coast

NC Birding Trail
NC Wildlife Resources Commission
1722 Mail Service Center
Raleigh, NC 27699-1722
(919) 604-5183
www.ncbirdingtrail.org

info@ncbirdingtrail.org

*I stopped by because of the
North Carolina Birding Trail.*

North Carolina
Birding Trail
mountains • piedmont • coast

NC Birding Trail
NC Wildlife Resources Commission
1722 Mail Service Center
Raleigh, NC 27699-1722
(919) 604-5183
www.ncbirdingtrail.org

info@ncbirdingtrail.org

*I stopped by because of the
North Carolina Birding Trail.*

North Carolina
Birding Trail
mountains • piedmont • coast

NC Birding Trail
NC Wildlife Resources Commission
1722 Mail Service Center
Raleigh, NC 27699-1722
(919) 604-5183
www.ncbirdingtrail.org

info@ncbirdingtrail.org

*I stopped by because of the
North Carolina Birding Trail.*

North Carolina
Birding Trail
mountains • piedmont • coast

NC Birding Trail
NC Wildlife Resources Commission
1722 Mail Service Center
Raleigh, NC 27699-1722
(919) 604-5183
www.ncbirdingtrail.org

info@ncbirdingtrail.org

*I stopped by because of the
North Carolina Birding Trail.*

North Carolina
Birding Trail
mountains • piedmont • coast

NC Birding Trail
NC Wildlife Resources Commission
1722 Mail Service Center
Raleigh, NC 27699-1722
(919) 604-5183
www.ncbirdingtrail.org

info@ncbirdingtrail.org

*I stopped by because of the
North Carolina Birding Trail.*

North Carolina
Birding Trail
mountains • piedmont • coast

NC Birding Trail
NC Wildlife Resources Commission
1722 Mail Service Center
Raleigh, NC 27699-1722
(919) 604-5183
www.ncbirdingtrail.org

info@ncbirdingtrail.org

*I stopped by because of the
North Carolina Birding Trail.*

North Carolina
Birding Trail
mountains • piedmont • coast

NC Birding Trail
NC Wildlife Resources Commission
1722 Mail Service Center
Raleigh, NC 27699-1722
(919) 604-5183
www.ncbirdingtrail.org

info@ncbirdingtrail.org

*I stopped by because of the
North Carolina Birding Trail.*

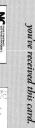

I'm using the North Carolina Birding Trail to locate great birding sites.

Please continue to care for your natural resources and I'll be back to use the Trail and patronize local businesses.

Please let the NC Birding Trail know you've received this card.

I'm using the North Carolina Birding Trail to locate great birding sites.

Please continue to care for your natural resources and I'll be back to use the Trail and patronize local businesses.

Please let the NC Birding Trail know you've received this card.

I'm using the North Carolina Birding Trail to locate great birding sites.

Please continue to care for your natural resources and I'll be back to use the Trail and patronize local businesses.

Please let the NC Birding Trail know you've received this card.

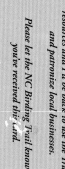

I'm using the North Carolina Birding Trail to locate great birding sites.

Please continue to care for your natural resources and I'll be back to use the Trail and patronize local businesses.

Please let the NC Birding Trail know you've received this card.

I'm using the North Carolina Birding Trail to locate great birding sites.

Please continue to care for your natural resources and I'll be back to use the Trail and patronize local businesses.

Please let the NC Birding Trail know you've received this card.